D0436688

In this current culture that is steeped in low expectations for morality and high expectations for appearances, *Made for This Moment* comes at just the right time. I'm proud of Madison, for not only writing this message but also living this message. This book is the perfect resource if you want insights on the struggles of those you love in their teens and twenties who often feel the tug of war between the world's ways and God's ways. And at the same time, this will boost your faith in the God who holds it all together and helps us stand strong in the face of tough choices. This fascinating story full of wisdom and biblical examples will stay with you long after the last page.

LYSA TERKEURST, #1 *New York Times* bestselling
author, president of Proverbs 31 Ministries

Our lives are made up of memories, and our memories are made up of moments. *Made for This Moment* will help you prepare for those courage-demanding moments so that they become memories you're proud of, learn from, and cherish. With wisdom beyond her years, Madi shares how she is able to stand firm in her convictions and values even amid pressure and the public eye. These pages are full of encouragement for any young woman who wants to live with greater confidence, courage, and commitment to God.

AUDREY ROLOFF, *New York Times* bestselling author of *A
Love Letter Life*, cofounder of The Marriage Journal

Madi is a leader who blazes trails for the next generation to live out their faith with courage and conviction. Her faith in public she lives out deeply in private.

JENNIE ALLEN, *New York Times* bestselling author of *Get Out
of Your Head*, founder and visionary of IF:Gathering

Made for This Moment by Madison Prewett is a wonderfully written book about making the most of every opportunity in your life. Madison uses her experiences as well as those of the biblical Esther as examples to help anyone recognize and prepare for those pivotal life-changing moments.

VICTORIA OSTEEN, *New York Times* bestselling
author, copastor of Lakewood Church

Made for This Moment combines Madi's honest (and fun) storytelling with wisdom that packs a punch. You'll walk away from reading this book empowered, equipped, and excited to live confidently in all God has for you!

DEMI-LEIGH TEBOW, Miss Universe 2017,
entrepreneur, and motivational speaker

Life has taught us that God can use the most unlikely setups to reveal his purposes. Madi is a beautiful and inspiring example of standing strong in our God-given identity in the midst of the fiery crucible of popularity and public opinion.

LISA BEVERE, *New York Times* bestselling author

The voice for a generation. In *Made for This Moment*, Madison shares her experience with humor, humility, authenticity, and vulnerability. The reader feels they are walking beside her in her journey and discovering the gold of her lessons learned in a practical and equipping way and discovers that they can apply these overcoming strategies to their own life situations. A key read "for such a time as this."

LoriANN V. LOWERY-BIGGERS, CEO of BellaVaughan, Inc., corporate
board director and former president of North America, Lloyd's
of London, Inc., and cohost of *The Leader's Panel* podcast

Madison Prewett is the real deal. *Made for This Moment* is raw and real and does not shy away from hard seasons in her life, all to help someone else out there. Madi has lived out these moments in her life with poise and discernment, and this book is proof of that. It will truly bless you today and going forward!

JEANINE AMAPOLA, Christian, YouTuber, podcaster, and Bible teacher

In a world that continually pressures us to compromise or even concede, Madison Prewett offers a courageous and needed perspective that you can stay relevant, stay kind, *and* still stand your ground.

LISA AND DAVID HUGHES

MADE FOR THIS
MOMENT

MADE FOR THIS
MOMENT

Standing Firm with
STRENGTH, GRACE, and COURAGE

MADISON PREWETT

ZONDERVAN
BOOKS

ZONDERVAN BOOKS

Made for This Moment
Copyright © 2021 by Madison Prewett

Requests for information should be addressed to:
Zondervan, *3900 Sparks Dr. SE, Grand Rapids, Michigan 49546*

Zondervan titles may be purchased in bulk for educational, business, fundraising, or sales promotional use. For information, please email SpecialMarkets@Zondervan.com.

ISBN 978-0-310-36318-7 (hardcover)
ISBN 978-0-310-36325-5 (audio)
ISBN 978-0-310-36320-0 (ebook)

All Scripture quotations, unless otherwise indicated, are taken from The Holy Bible, New International Version®, NIV®. Copyright © 1973, 1978, 1984, 2011 by Biblica, Inc.® Used by permission of Zondervan. All rights reserved worldwide. www.Zondervan.com. The "NIV" and "New International Version" are trademarks registered in the United States Patent and Trademark Office by Biblica, Inc.®

Scripture quotations marked KJV are taken from the King James Version. Public domain.

Scripture quotations marked MSG are taken from *THE MESSAGE*. Copyright © 1993, 2002, 2018 by Eugene H. Peterson. Used by permission of NavPress. All rights reserved. Represented by Tyndale House Publishers, Inc.

Scripture quotations marked NLT are taken from the Holy Bible, New Living Translation. © 1996, 2004, 2015 by Tyndale House Foundation. Used by permission of Tyndale House Publishers, Inc., Carol Stream, Illinois 60188. All rights reserved.

Any internet addresses (websites, blogs, etc.) and telephone numbers in this book are offered as a resource. They are not intended in any way to be or imply an endorsement by Zondervan, nor does Zondervan vouch for the content of these sites and numbers for the life of this book.

All rights reserved. No part of this publication may be reproduced, stored in a retrieval system, or transmitted in any form or by any means—electronic, mechanical, photocopy, recording, or any other—except for brief quotations in printed reviews, without the prior permission of the publisher.

The information in this book has been carefully researched by the author, and is intended to be a source of information only. Readers are urged to consult with their physicians or other professional advisors to address specific medical issues. The author and the publisher assume no responsibility for any injuries suffered or damages or losses incurred during or as a result of the use or application of the information contained herein.

This is a work of nonfiction. Some names and identifying details have been changed to protect the privacy of individuals mentioned in this work.

Published in association with the literary agency of The Fedd Agency, Post Office Box 341973, Austin, TX 78734.

Cover design and photo: Micah Kandros
Interior design: Sara Colley

Printed in the United States of America

21 22 23 24 25 26 27 28 29 30 31 32 /LSC/ 14 13 12 11 10 9 8 7 6 5 4 3 2 1

To the woman who embodied strength, grace, and courage to my sisters and me: my beautiful mother, Tonya Prewett. You have loved me and encouraged me through my lowest and darkest times and cheered me on and celebrated me through my greatest moments. I wouldn't be who I am today without the prayer, support, and wisdom from you and Dad. Thank you for praying for me and believing in me when no one else did.

To the women who have shared their stories with me—the heartbreaks, struggles, hopes, fears, and dreams—I write this book for you. I know you long to know your worth and seek the courage to stand up for what you believe in. I pray through each page you feel empowered, encouraged, and enlightened as you realize that the true hero that lies within these pages is you. You were made for this moment.

CONTENTS

FOREWORD

S tudies show that the average person's greatest fear is public speaking. Not death, but speaking in front of a crowd! (Let that one sink in.) While I grew up in the public spotlight along with my family, I can't imagine what it would be like to be on stage in front of cameras capturing my dating life and most vulnerable moments on live television—in front of millions. Of course, that's what happened to my friend Madi Prewett when she reached the finale of *The Bachelor* in season 24.

I met Madi at Passion Conference in 2019, shortly after her time on *The Bachelor*. However, it wasn't until my husband, Christian, and I moved to Auburn, Alabama, Madi's hometown, that I truly got to know her and her story. It did not take me long to discover what much of America learned about her on national television— that she has a strong personal faith that is real and vibrant and that she seeks to honor God in all her decisions, even when the eyes of the world are watching. As our friendship has deepened, I have come to know Madi as a strong, sensitive, and caring person. She has held true to her identity and her beliefs even under the scrutiny of the spotlight and continues to be a role model for young women around the world.

In *Made for This Moment*, Madi gives us all a peek inside the person we saw only a glimpse of when she walked away from *The Bachelor*. Madi shares how she was able to stand up for her faith in front of millions and make a conscious decision to honor God when no one was watching. In these pages, you will see what it means to be a person of character and to live each day aware that every decision—small and large—matters.

I'm really excited that you've picked up Madi's book. I hope it will be like a shot of wisdom and hope for your soul, as it was for mine. I am inspired and encouraged by Madi's story—and her conviction that the way we respond to pressure matters, but the way we prepare matters just as much. Just like Esther in the Bible, Madi faced her "big moment" and didn't falter in her convictions. And my prayer is that as you read *Made for This Moment*, you, like Esther, will realize that God has chosen you—yes, you!—for such a time as this.

Sadie Robertson Huff

INTRODUCTION

A moment. It can change everything. It can give you the freedom to go higher, or it can rob you of all you thought you had. A moment can make you, or it can take from you.

When we gather and throw a big celebration, we are creating a moment. When we take photos, we are capturing moments. Some moments are bigger than others, and some may be considered small moments, but they all matter because together they create the sum of a life. The big moments are attainable because of the small moments. How you spend your moments alone matters. How you steward your smaller moments matters. How you respond to the bigger and pressure-filled moments matters. That is the power of a moment. It can make or break you. It can build you or destroy you. It can change your mindset for a day. It can change your goals for a year. It can change your life forever. Just one moment.

What I want you to know is that whatever moment you are in right now is the moment you were made for.

In this book I want to share with you the moments that have shaped who I am and who I am becoming, so that you will be encouraged in your own life-shaping moments. I want to invite you into my most vulnerable and painful moments so that you will know it's possible to stand strong through your broken and rough moments.

When a moment that challenges you comes, will you stand firm in who you are? When a moment that could change you arrives, will you be ready? When a moment of opportunity shows up at your door, will you be prepared? When the moment of pressure hits, how will you respond? How we respond to pressure matters, but how we prepare matters just as much. In these moments, "winging it" rarely cuts it. The time we set aside to prepare for the moments that will test our limits sets the tone for how we will respond.

So what can we do? We must invest in our own moment-making disciplines. It's time to ready ourselves for the challenges of the world. We must face our pasts, engage in the worthy struggle for our identities, and fight comparison with confidence. We have to prepare for pressure. It's time to anticipate the moments ahead and not simply wait for notifications to light up our phones. It's time to lean into that shaky courage that comes when you face something scary but you know you're not alone. It's time to discover who you are so you can walk confidently in all God has for you. It's time to rise up, take your position, and get ready to fight for your moment.

In *Made for This Moment*, we will explore how to be ready for times in life that make you, challenge you, and change you. No matter your age, ethnicity, job title, or past or current struggles, you matter and your moments matter because they are the makings of your life. Your time has come! Consider this your invitation to step out and live up the one life you have to live.

Over the last year, I have had my fair share of make-or-break moments! In the midst of them, I have been encouraged and challenged by the words of Esther 4:14: "Who knows but that you have come to your royal position for such a time as this?" Or as we might say today, "Maybe you were made for this moment."

CHAPTER 1

COURAGE FOR YOUR MOMENT

Believing You Were Made for This

My heart was pounding. I was trembling. There was a knot in my stomach. I'm pretty sure I had already sweat through the hot-pink dress I was wearing. I had no idea what was about to go down. All I knew was that I was about to go on live television with millions of people watching. What would I be asked? How would I respond? I had rehearsed hundreds of times. I was ready. Or was I? I paced. I prayed. I reapplied my lipstick. I prayed some more. I took deep breaths. My heart felt like it was beating out of my chest. Fear of the what-ifs consumed my mind. What if someone accuses me of something I didn't do? What if the audience cheers against me? Could I do this? I could run away. I could back out. How did I get here?

I had faced so much to arrive at this moment. I had fallen in love, worked through conflict, publicly taken heat about my personal choices at levels I'd never expected, and ended a relation-ship. Now I was on the verge of a second chance at this relationship.

It was *The Bachelor* finale, the final episode where the Bachelor and his final choice tell the world how they really feel—at the end of the line, after the final rose. It is the only live show of the season. And it is always the most watched.

I had made it to this moment. I should be excited, right?

My producer walked in to tell me that it was time. The sound-man attached my microphone, and I was led backstage. There was no turning back now. I could see the crowd of people in the audi-ence. My heart was beating so hard I thought everyone around me could hear it. I tried to tell myself I had no reason to worry. God was with me in this moment. I had prayed about this. Everything leading up to this moment had been so promising. Now all I had to do was walk on that stage, remember what I had rehearsed in my mind hundreds of times, and speak with confidence. Easy.

But nothing about the next few minutes was easy. I could never have anticipated what was to come. I walked out on stage and took my seat next to the Bachelor, Peter Weber. Neither of us knew exactly what would happen. All we knew was that we wanted this moment to be real, raw, and authentic. Since this was the first live show of the season, it was our moment to be ourselves, to share what we were feeling, and figure out what we wanted to do moving forward.

The host of the show welcomed us and began asking a series of questions. Everyone in the crowd was silent, watching and waiting to see what I would say and what we would decide to do. I saw the large camera crew making sure they captured every angle and every reaction from me and from those all around me. As I sat there in that moment, I remembered the words my mom had written in a letter that she hid in my suitcase the night before the finale: "You are stronger than you realize, Madi. Do not let anything catch you off guard. If anyone blindsides you, keep your composure and respond with grace and confidence."

Though I had played out many scenarios in my mind, I wasn't prepared for what came next.

Words came at me so fast, I couldn't even get a word in. I was stunned by the accusations and hurtful comments, words that felt like an attack against my character and convictions. Words sent to berate me. This was the last thing I expected.

My heart skipped a beat. Maybe two. It all happened so fast. There was so much I wanted to explain and say, but we were on stage for only a short time, maybe ten minutes.

I wish I could put into words what I felt in that moment. The weight of the words that were directed at me. The pain of feeling misunderstood. The heaviness I felt in my chest as I realized that millions were watching. My parents were watching. My friends were watching. The world was watching. Under most circumstances, my initial response to criticism is to be defensive. To fight back. To retaliate. Somehow, miraculously, I held my tongue. I kept my composure. I felt in that moment, I had to know when to speak and when to be silent. I came in prepared to tell my side of the story. There was so much people didn't see or understand. This was my time to explain everything, to tell the world how I really felt.

Words formed in my mouth, but I knew I had to restrain them. I wanted to cry, but knew I had to be strong. I wanted to run off the stage, but I knew I had to stay. I felt I was in a lose-lose situation. Having only ten minutes on live television, with no plan, I thought this was my time to share my heart and let people see all of me, the real me. But what could I do? If I cried, I would be seen as weak. If I fought back, I would be seen as angry and disrespectful. All I knew to do was to keep silent, hold my composure as best I could, and smile. But as I tried to form a smile, my lips quivered and I knew tears were soon to follow.

I remember thinking, "Where are you, God? I could really use your help right about now. This is the moment when you come in and fix everything."

But God had other plans. Plans I couldn't understand. Not yet anyway. Something much bigger was going on behind the scenes that I did not understand in that moment. As this book unfolds, I will reveal more about this story and many others that challenged my courage and ability to stand strong under pressure.

Sometimes it's not the words we say that show the depth of our hearts, but rather the ones we choose not to say.

When I think back to that moment, I think of the courage it took not to retaliate. Courage comes in many forms. Sometimes it's speaking out, taking a stand, raising your voice. But sometimes it's knowing when to show restraint. Sometimes it's not the words we say that show the depth of our hearts, but rather the ones we choose not to say.

Minutes felt like hours but passed like seconds. I looked at the clock and saw how much time was left before we would be ushered off the stage. The tension in the room could be cut with a knife.

As soon as the filming ended, I ran backstage, trying my best to hold it together, but as soon as I turned the corner to head out the door, where there were no more crowds or cameras, I broke down completely. Several people had tried to stop me from running off, but I kept running until I found a single bathroom to lock myself in and be alone so that I could gather my thoughts. I kept rehashing what had just happened and felt so embarrassed, humiliated, and more hurt than I had ever been.

For everyone else this was entertainment. They watched the

finale and then went on with their lives. But for me it was real life. It wasn't just a TV show. It wasn't something I could turn off and move on from.

It felt like no one could possibly understand what I was feeling. I felt hurt and alone. So I hid in my single-stall bathroom. And cried.

"You are stronger than you realize, Madi." My mom's words kept coming back to me. I knew I needed to call my mom. If anyone could help me understand the intensity of what I had just been through, it would be her. As soon as I got back to the hotel room, I called her. She answered, and before I could say a word, she said, "I told you that you were strong." I began to cry because I felt anything but strong. She continued, "Do not waste one second worrying about what just happened. It will serve a greater purpose than you can imagine." Even though I did not understand it all in that moment, I trusted her.

She was right; it did serve a greater purpose. I could never have predicted where my life would go in the next year. Dots were being connected that I couldn't see or understand at the time. But God did. He had a bigger purpose in mind. It was in that painful, lonely, and unknown season of life that I discovered the courage I needed to step out and begin. Courage to begin writing the book you now hold in your hands. Courage to begin speaking to young people about their worth and purpose. Courage to walk in the direction of my calling.

Each of the chapters in this book will unfold more of the story that led to this pivotal moment, *The Bachelor* finale. I want to share with you what I've learned about having strength, grace, and courage in the face of adversity and pressure. I don't claim to know everything there is to know about being brave and courageous. I have tripped up and caved in plenty of times. But the last year of my life has caused me to take a deeper look at who I am and who I want to be. And if your experience as a young woman in today's world is anything like mine—and I don't mean *Bachelor* finale experiences, but the pressures and struggles that attack your confidence and courage—I want to help you wrestle with some soul-shaping questions that I believe are important to ask as we look to our futures. How do we stand firm and stay strong in a world that tries to pull us down, pressure us, and label us? How do we keep our standards high and our roots deep so that when the tough moments hit, we are prepared?

With the speed of our lives, the instant nature of our communication, and the constant pressure to present the perfect image, it's not easy to find our footing on the fly. If, at a moment's notice, something challenges who you are, how can you be prepared to stand firm? Are these moments all about trusting your gut and hoping you don't majorly screw up?

When I think about that night of the finale, I had some real choices to make in a moment of immense pressure. If I had acted out of instinct, I might have let loose some words I would have later regretted. Yes, I wanted to cater to that impulse, but I dug deep and drew up a stronger version of myself than I thought possible. How on earth did I make it to that point? The short answer: It took courage. A lot of courage.

Maybe you're wondering, "So, Madi, how do you prepare for unexpected moments? How do you stand courageous when you feel like running away? When you feel overpowered?" That's what I want to unpack in the following pages. I love a quote by Bethany Hamilton that captures what I want to share with you: "Courage doesn't mean you don't get afraid. Courage means you don't let fear stop you."[1] You and I may have very different stories since the pressures we face take on many different forms. But those challenges leave all the same feelings on the inside. I want to share how you can be strong and courageous no matter what you have been through and no matter what you are facing.

Courage in the Face of Fear

What are you most afraid of?

Fear can cripple you. It can rob you. And it almost always leaves you with a nauseating feeling in the pit of your stomach. Fear can keep us from relationships, careers, successes, and dreams and has the power to prevent us from living the life we desire.

We often let our minds become consumed with negative possibilities in life. Sometimes I think it's easy, as women, to live in a constant state of fear. Fear concerning our future, our health, our finances, our families. Fear of what others think about us. Fear of the what-ifs. *What if my boyfriend stops loving me? What if I'm unable to have children? What if I can't pay for college? Pay my rent? What if I'm not strong? Smart? Pretty? What if I'm not included? What if I don't measure up? What if I'm not enough?*

Do you struggle with these types of worries? Do you find yourself constantly battling fear? I don't know what your fears look like, but I used to be consumed with what other people thought about me. In school, I was afraid of answering questions in class for fear that I would say something stupid. As an athlete, I was afraid of underperforming, fearing that others would think I was not as good as they had hoped. As a friend, I was afraid of vocalizing my opinions or making plans for the group for fear that I might be overlooked and passed over. In relationships, I was afraid to commit and give my heart, dreading being rejected and others seeing that I was unwanted or replaceable. For many years, this fear trapped me and kept me from reaching my full potential. How often does fear of what other people think stop you from doing something or being your true self?

Fear of the what-ifs have always been a huge struggle for me. I like to plan and be in control so that I don't fail or make mistakes along the way. When I left for *The Bachelor*, I had no way of knowing whether I would be gone for one week or ten weeks. Fearful thoughts immediately bombarded me: What if I'm rejected for who I am? What if the other girls don't like me? What if I get my heart broken? What if I'm misunderstood? What if I'm not strong enough to stay true to myself?

Usually when I had thoughts like these, my mom would snap me back into focus, quickly reminding me of who I am and encouraging me with the truth and promises of God's Word.

But one of the scary parts of this journey was that I had to step into it alone. I wouldn't have my mom to call, my friends to text, or my dad to cry to. Not seeing my family or talking to them would be hard since I talk to them almost every day, especially my mom. Whether it was calling her about what I should wear, needing her to help me with my work and emails, or simply to talk, I rarely went a day without talking to her. But thankfully, she gave me a few pieces of wisdom to take with me.

As I prepared to leave for the show, my mom handed me a stack of letters, one for each day. The problem was she had no idea how many days I would be gone. So she wrote until she felt led to stop. Forty-one letters. It must have taken her forever to write all those! I was moved to tears. This was the best gift someone could give me. I knew I would be in an environment where the people around me wouldn't always understand me, or I would be in situations where I wouldn't know what to do and I wouldn't have my phone to call my mom. These letters were her way of being there with me, giving me the inspiration, motivation, and advice I needed each day to remind me of who I am, what's inside me, and that I'm not alone. Each day as I read one of her letters, it gave me the courage I needed for that day, one day at a time. The letters, all forty-one of them, lasted until hometown dates. Then they ran out. The day I opened the last envelope was the day I would see my family again for the first time . . . in forty-one days. Wow!

I want to share what my mom wrote in the first letter.

She told me about a story she heard years ago about the relationship between a mother eagle and her babies. The mother eagle spends weeks preparing the nest and getting food for her babies. The eaglets do nothing on their own. They stay within the nest, usually under the protection of their mom. She watches over them, shelters them, and feeds them, day after day. The time finally comes when she knows what she has to do. I'm sure she fears what could happen, but it's time. She knows that until the eaglets learn to fly on their own, they will fail to understand the purpose and privilege of being an eagle.

Until you face your fear with courage, you won't be able to access your greatest potential: soaring.

Mom encouraged me with these words on the card: "The nest was necessary, but it was temporary, because in time, the nest becomes a hindrance. The scary places will reveal things you never thought you had inside of you, Madi. How you handle the uncomfortable times, the push—matters. Trust God even when it doesn't make sense. You don't belong in the nest. You were created to soar."

These words carried me through many difficult and hard moments. The story reminded me that through the pain and the struggle, I was growing, experiencing, and continuing to learn how to flap my wings. It reminded me not to resent pain, or "the push," but to trust that in the struggle and resistance is where I learn to soar.

I have met many people who have been trapped in their own nests and haven't mustered the courage they need to spread their wings and fly because they fear what-ifs: What if I fall? What if I'm not ready? What if the nest is better, safer, than whatever unknown is out there? What if I'm not as good as the others?

Whatever your fears are, it is time to face them head on! It's time to tell your fears how strong you are. Look your fear straight in the face, and do whatever it is you're afraid of right in front of it. Once you do, you will see that the worst scenario you imagined never really existed at all. Whether through our own will or with the help of another, we need the courage to push ourselves into the unknown, as scary as it may be. This is where our wings are built—this is where courage is developed. And you will discover that you have what you need to soar!

Courage in the Face of Opposition

In recent months, I have felt strongly that God is raising up women of today to stand firm and carry an unshakable and unbreakable spirit of courage, using the skills and resources they possess to make an impact on this generation. There will always be people or situations that try to limit our impact, silence our voice, and keep us from our purpose. We need courage to stand up to people who oppose us, not only for ourselves but also for those who look up to us, whether they be our siblings, our friends, our coworkers, or strangers on social media.

But what is the source of courage? Where does it come from? Why do some seem to be more courageous than others? We can find the courage we need in our relationship with God and his Spirit within us. He promises never to leave or forsake us, and that should make us brave! I discovered that I could rely on God to give me courage when I most needed it, and when I called on him, I knew his Spirit was with me.

Earlier I shared a moment when I embraced true, godly courage: showing restraint and remaining silent. Yet some moments in life require us to speak out and use our voices. True God-honoring courage is having the wisdom to discern when to speak and when to be silent. There is a story in the Bible of a woman who is the perfect example of someone who rose in courage and used her voice, even in the face of opposition. The book of Esther tells the story of an unlikely queen who, in spite of fear and great personal risk, spoke out boldly to save her people from destruction.

Esther didn't seek out the position of queen. The position sought her. The king had been rejected by his queen at the time, Vashti. She had been summoned one evening to present herself to the king and his guests, but Vashti refused to come, feeling it would be beneath her to entertain the king and his friends with her beauty. This defiance infuriated the king, and he issued a decree to search for a new queen. Esther, a Jew in exile, was one of the women under consideration.

As we read about Esther's upbringing and history, we learn that she was an orphan, with no family to call her own except one cousin, Mordecai. Young and away from her home country, Esther was taken into the royal courts. Here, with all the other women, she was primped and prodded and run through the beautification routine. She was pleasing to the king's eye and won his favor. The royal crown was placed on her head and she was declared queen. Yet Esther concealed an important detail about her identity—her Jewish heritage.

Upon overhearing Haman, one of the king's advisors, plotting to destroy the Jews, her own people, Esther had a choice to make. Would she confront the king and reveal her heritage in an attempt to save a nation, or would she suffer in silence?

Esther needed to save her people, but it would require incredible courage. Anyone who went into the king's presence without being summoned could be executed (for this was a rule during this time), and the king had not requested her presence in a month. Of all the Jews in the empire, she alone had access to the king, but approaching him uninvited could be her death sentence.

Mordecai pleaded with her to speak to the king on behalf of the Jewish people, reminding her of God's purposeful timing by saying, "If you remain silent at this time, relief and deliverance for the Jews will arise from another place, but you and your father's family will perish. And who knows but that you have come to your royal position for such a time as this?" (Esther 4:14).

The biggest decision of Esther's life came down to this one moment. Esther understood that her promotion wasn't just for her personal pleasure. She had been put in the palace to serve a great purpose. She had a choice to make: to play it safe for herself personally and gamble the risk of what might happen next or to brave the unknown, come what may. That was all it took to summon the courage needed to fulfill her mission.

> Sometimes being courageous means braving the battles no one else is willing to fight.

Sometimes being courageous means braving the battles no one else is willing to fight.

Putting on her best royal robes, Esther approached the king, unsummoned, and eventually told him of Haman's plot against her people and made her request for help. In a miraculous turn of events, the king chose not to execute her and ordered that the Jewish people be saved.

Esther had to overcome fear and battle opposition. Even though times are different in today's world than they were thousands of years ago, Esther still had to battle the same issues we face today, and she was called to rise in courage as you and I are. When Esther was up against the toughest challenge of her life, she drew up boldness and courage to speak out against the oppression of her people because those characteristics were core to who she was. She responded to her circumstances from a position of strength. While we might think her courage to approach the king was just an adrenaline-fueled moment, a closer look reveals something crucial: she was prepared for this moment long before it arrived.

Even though this story was written thousands of years ago, many of the struggles Esther faced are relatable to what you and I face today. Esther had to decide whether to keep her faith a secret to protect her family, face opposition and attacks for her beliefs, and experience the fears and loneliness of knowing she had to take a stand for her people even if it cost her her life. But no matter what came, Esther used each moment as an opportunity to cultivate strength, grace, and courage. Her courage, along with her preparation, changed the course of history for generations to come.

We will all have tipping points, moments that change everything. While we don't know exactly when they will come, we can come to those moments fully prepared. Behind every courageous moment are hundreds of other moments that cultivated that courage.

As young women today, we need to cultivate courage from within to face the moments ahead of us. I believe God is raising up Esthers all over the world who will take their stand and be a voice.

Yes, we will have to battle fear and face opposition. But don't grow battle-weary; your time is now, and God will give you strength!

Cultivating courage means that rather than letting obstacles hinder us from our purpose, we prepare our hearts and minds to let the pain, fear, and opposition be a chapter in our story and not the ending. So, I ask you, what will you do when you are called to be courageous? Will you stand up when needed? What will you do when your moment comes? Whether your moment seems big or small, whether it will define a generation or make all the difference just to you, be ready. The best news is that God has empowered you for exactly this. He has placed his courage inside you so that when the next challenge, large or small, comes calling, you can know with confidence that *you were made for this!*

Challenges on Courage

1. Can you recall a time when you were rejected and insecurities creeped in? Could this be when your courage was stripped away? If you regularly deal with fear, name it and confront it honestly, but don't stay stuck in it.

2. Say yes if a moment arrives and there is an urging inside you and a peace in your heart. Say yes even if you're terrified to the bone. Stepping into the unknown can be scary, but greatness is rarely achieved in comfort—it will require stepping out in courage, even if it's scary and no one else understands.

3. Trust the push. Find people who will remind you of your identity and push you toward your purpose. Their push might be challenging, but it will help you keep going even when everything in you wants to give up. Trust the push and know that just because you said yes to something doesn't mean it will be easy. Typically, it gets harder from the moment you say yes. But you're ready and you can do it. Believe in yourself and ask God daily for the courage to persevere.

4. Don't be afraid to stand out. But pray for wisdom to know when to speak out and when to be silent.

CHAPTER 2

READY OR NOT

Becoming in Private the Person
Who Will Make You Proud in Public

It was the last thing I wanted, but I couldn't stop myself: the Chick-fil-A cashier saw me cry.

It happened like this. My phone rang. "This is it!" I thought, "This is the call I've been waiting for and praying about." I had tears in my eyes because of the amount of prayer that had gone into waiting for this one phone call. Before I could even grab my food from the window, I had to pull out of the drive-through line because I couldn't miss this call. I knew deep down that God was calling me to a place of unfamiliarity. I knew God was calling me to step out in faith. Typically, I would do so without hesitation, but this was different. This would be bold, even for me. This decision came with a cost, a pressure, and a fear that I had never experienced before. I clearly saw what would lie ahead of me if I said yes. I would be misunderstood, judged, and become the hottest topic of gossip around town . . . not to mention the internet.

I was fearful of what others would say and how I would be judged and possibly attacked. I didn't feel like anyone would ever truly understand. Shoot, I didn't even understand why this was the direction I felt God was leading me! Selfishly, I thought, "God, I want to be courageous in *my* plans and in *my* timing!" Even though this opportunity wasn't what I expected, I had a peace and a nervous excitement.

I drove back home, chicken sandwich-less. For hours I sat in my car and stared at the garage door. I couldn't believe I had just said yes to stepping into something I knew would change my life forever. God showed me and reminded me of all the times throughout my life that had prepared me for this moment. All the tough blows, heartbreaks, and lonely nights did something deep within me that I hadn't realized—those moments built within me strength, toughness, grit, and courage for what I was about to face.

Not Perfect, but Prepared

To some, what I felt God was calling me to may not seem like a big deal. But to me, it was life changing. A lot of people would assume that stepping into a reality TV show would be easy or that I did it to promote myself. I understand all that. But to help you understand more about why it was so difficult for me, let me tell you a little more of my story.

I grew up in a Christian home and had a deep connection with God that started at a young age and continued until my early high school years. As a teenager, I fell under the traps of comparison and placing my identity in the wrong things. I found myself seeking attention, worth, and acceptance in anything but God. My identity was found in what I wore, the boys who pursued me, the sports I played and trophies I won, and how many likes I got on Instagram. These all left me unsatisfied, empty, and confused. I went into college with the same struggles and issues. Then one night I was invited to a small group, not knowing a soul. I decided to go all in with Jesus that night. And I left that small group with a new friend—one of my best friends to this day—as well as a forever-changed heart. This moment changed a lot for me.

For the next five years, I served as a college leader at my church and went through my church's seminary and leadership program. I then started Bible college through my church and graduated with a certificate in ministry the same year I graduated Auburn University with my degree in Communications. After graduation, I went on to work as a foster parent recruiter, while also continuing to serve at my church on the creative team.

Let me paint you a picture of what I imagined my life would look like and the direction it was headed: I expected to marry a pastor and be content with my family of five sitting up front at every church service and taking our yearly mission trips. I even thought we would possibly live overseas as full-time missionaries— whatever God called us to! My life would be one of those two scenarios, not too much outside of that. I had gladly accepted that as God's will for me. Except that wasn't God's will for my life. I had limited God by putting him in the box of my own dreams and expectations.

So how did I go from dating a pastor and graduating from seminary school to saying yes to going on *The Bachelor*? To be honest, at first I had reservations. I felt that the entire world would condemn and judge me because of my faith and standards and that no one would understand why I would go on the show. I also felt like the church would cast me aside for going on a secular dating TV show. I would be left somewhere in the middle, feeling misunderstand by everyone.

I sat in my car after I arrived home from Chick-fil-A, thinking about how I even got here. Getting this call from *The Bachelor*, asking me to be a contestant on their show, and praying about whether I should say yes or no, I reflected on how it all began.

I remember the exact day: I was at my friend's house and we were supposed to have a small group Bible study. We were going through a book on relationships called *Single, Dating, Engaged, Married* by Ben Stuart. The ironic part of this small group was that I started it while dating someone, then was close to getting engaged, but instead broke up, leaving me in the single category. I felt like I was literally living out the book I was reading. On this particular night, I walked into the house and noticed that no one had their books. Instead, the TV was on and everyone was crouched over, biting their nails and intensely watching something. Confused, I walked in and sat down and noticed they were watching *The Bachelor*. I had never seen the show. The night ended up being centered on *Bachelor* talk and popcorn. After the episode ended, two of the girls looked at me and said with confidence, "You should go on the show." I thought it was a joke. I looked at them and I laughingly said, "Y'all are crazy!"

Months passed and I had forgotten about that night. One day at the gym while I was on the treadmill, I looked down at my phone and noticed that I was getting a call from a California number and thought it was odd, so I answered. "Hello?"

"Hi. Is this Madison? We were wondering if you were still interested in being on this next season of *The Bachelor*."

I stepped off the treadmill. At first I thought they had the wrong Madison. I thought, "Wait! I didn't apply for *The Bachelor*. How in the world did they get my informat—." Then it hit me. The girls from my small group had applied for me without telling me! "What do I say now?" I wanted to be respectful.

She spoke up again, "Hello? Madison, can you hear me?"

I quickly assured her, "Yes, I am still here! I just wasn't expecting this at all. Can you email me some more details? I will think about it."

Truth is, I did not intend to think about it. I already knew my answer to that question. Going on the show wouldn't make sense for me. I immediately called my mom, thinking she would agree with me that I should say no, but she insisted that I shouldn't close the door without taking some time to think and pray about it. In the background I could hear my sister Mallory running around, screaming, "This is so cool! Madi, you have to do it!"

I tried not to think about it, but I couldn't stop. The decision was constantly on my mind. I wanted to treat this opportunity like it wasn't a big deal, but deep down inside I was freaking out and wanted to tell all my best friends about it! As I continued to pray about it, I had enough peace to at least begin the process.

Throughout the interview process, my family and I prayed about what I should do. We continued to receive peace at each step. I prayed day and night for months. I dedicated twenty-one days to prayer, with the intent of getting the answer I needed. I asked seven people—my closest friends, family, and mentors—to stand with me in prayer for direction, clarity, and wisdom on what to do. Throughout those twenty-one days, the peace, signs, and words God gave me left me without a doubt. I knew what I was supposed to do.

On day twenty-one of prayer, I broke down in tears. "God, I feel this is where you are leading me, but I'm scared. I'm terrified. I don't know if I can do it." As I finished praying, my pastor came up to me, and without knowing any details of what was truly going on and what I was praying for, he looked at me and said with confidence, "Whatever you are praying for, I just want you to know I am confident that you can do it and you have people around you who believe in you." It was the exact affirmation I needed to hear in that moment. I felt a peace come over me that I will never be able to put into words. I knew in that moment that if they called to ask me to be an official contestant, I wouldn't be confused, doubtful, or uncertain. I would know exactly how to respond: with a surprising yes.

Saying yes to *The Bachelor*, or rather saying yes to the unfamiliar and uncomfortable, didn't come easily. Saying yes came from a place of trust and peace. I trusted that this was where God was leading me. And I was choosing to walk in courage, even though every voice around me (and even inside me) was fearful of what could happen.

Like the person who is "it" in a game of hide-and-seek, these defining moments in our lives call out to us, "Ready or not, here I come." My guess is that your instinct is to yell back, "Not ready! Definitely *not* ready! Give me a minute to find a better hiding place." This was what I wanted to say so badly, but God was leading me out into the wide open.

Maybe, like me, you have been called to step up to the plate or called to a task that you don't feel fit for or good enough for. Maybe you have experienced so many disappointments that you fear to hope and dream again. Instead, you play it safe so that you don't get hurt and you don't hurt anyone else. Maybe you have been in a moment that demanded courage, but you didn't rise up because you were too worried about what other people would think. I get it. I have been there too. And let me make it clear: I'm not perfect and don't have all the answers, but I have learned courage through mistakes, failure, heartbreak, loss, pain, and a lot of pressure.

I've learned the power of preparation and the importance of the process. I've had to learn how to break free from my past to be able to step into my potential. I have had to step into the unknown, just trusting the peace I felt. I had to step into a situation that required courage, letting go of my personal dreams and expectations. But courage didn't just come out of nowhere. It was built through years of failure, disappointments, and fears. It was built when no one was around.

I have learned that how you prepare in private will determine how you perform in public. **In unseen moments, waiting moments, and painful moments, you are preparing for the moments that will shape the course of your life.** This is where growth happens—hidden away from the spotlight. It's in the long days of waiting that character is forged. It is in these moments when pain turns to strength and endurance.

Privacy Please!

I had a friend in high school whose parents would remove the door to her bedroom every time she got in trouble. This was her parents' way of punishing her so that she would learn from her mistakes. She hated it so much. Why? Because she wanted privacy. We all want our privacy. Those are the moments we can be who we want to be without any judgment from others. Those are the moments we can walk in freedom. When I say freedom, yes, I mean walk around naked, not worrying about who is looking at us! We can sing loud in the shower, talk to ourselves in the mirror, dream up fake rom-com scenarios, and have time to ourselves. This is what many of us envision when we hear "Can I have some privacy, please?"

But privacy is more than just alone time to sing loud and dance crazy. Our private life shapes us for our public life. It is in the private time, the alone time, the quiet and unseen moments, that strength and courage are built, confidence is cultivated and grown, and endurance is established. Private time can be filled with waiting, hiding, pain, preparation, and a whole lot of growth.

Private time is so important. Who you are when no one is watching is who you will be when everyone is watching. Private decisions are underrated by many in our world today, and public decisions are often overrated. Public moments are praised and private moments passed over. Yet if we want to be moment-makers and not moment-breakers, we should embrace the private time, because it is there that the most courageous decisions are made. You may not get a pat on the back or a trophy for your courageous private decisions, but through each of them, you will be getting ready to stand firm with courage in your public decisions.

> Who you are when no one is watching is who you will be when everyone is watching.

You may be asking yourself, "What do I do to prepare for these moments? How do I embrace private time and steward it well? How do I build my integrity and strength?" Throughout this chapter we will unpack different private life moments and how to embrace them. I want to note here that true integrity isn't accomplished by impressing people on the outside; it is about doing the impressive hard work on the inside. In private you invest, build, and prepare for when you will hear a mean comment about your outfit or body or experience a friendship fallout, a breakup, or tempting moments with your boyfriend or peers.

When we read through the New Testament in the Bible, we see that one of Jesus's common practices was to withdraw to spend time alone with God. In a way these were crucial moments that prepared Christ for what he knew was coming: the cross. If the Son of God needed private moments to withdraw and be alone with God to strengthen and encourage his spirit, how much more do we?

In Matthew chapter 4, Jesus prays and fasts for forty days. That sounds a little intense to many of us, but Jesus was preparing for what he knew would soon come. The big moments in life require more intense preparation. And to be prepared, we have to create time alone with God.

People often ask me how I've been able to have so much strength and willpower when it comes to staying true to myself and my convictions, especially in high-pressure environments. I always respond, "The strength that you see in public is directly connected to the decisions I made in private." What I mean is that your toughest decisions in life and most pressure-filled moments will require a lot of strength and courage. Yet strength and courage don't pop up only when all eyes are on you; they are developed in the moments when no one is around. So I think we all need more "Privacy please!" moments so that we can be ready to rise in courage no matter what life throws our way.

Prepared in the Waiting

You've heard it said, "Patience is a virtue." If you are anything like me, this axiom does not make you happy. Because I am an impatient person, I hate waiting. I want to *do*. I want to act. And I want it now! Is it just me? I hate waiting for the light to turn green. I hate waiting in long lines for coffee. I hate waiting for the confused person in front of me to figure out what they want to order. Maybe you find yourself here—not literally in one of those scenarios, but maybe you are waiting for God to reveal the next step for your future, or waiting for that guy to finally ask you out, or waiting for the perfect job opportunity.

As much as I hate waiting, there is one thing God has continued to reveal to me in those hard-fought waiting seasons: what I am waiting on is not as valuable as the person I am becoming in the meantime. At first I didn't want to believe that. I was impatient and wanted to blame my waiting on someone else. God. My boyfriend. My family. It was so much easier to look outward rather than inward. It was easier to be frustrated and mad at the situation rather than learn and grow from it. I would often think, "Not only am I waiting on my blessing, but I'm watching everyone else get theirs!"

> What you are waiting on is not as valuable as the person you are becoming in the meantime.

But God spoke that same phrase to me over and over. That's when it hit me: I am the only one who can keep me from what God has for me. No one can take my purpose or potential from me. No one can rob me of God's plans for my life. Except me. My selfishness, laziness, pride, and defensive spirit can keep me from receiving and stepping into the promises God has for me. I don't always understand why certain situations turn out the way they do, or why it sometimes takes so long to get what you have been praying for. What I do know is that I can either choose to trust him or try to control it all myself—I can't do both.

So I choose trust. I choose to learn. I choose to grow. I hope you will too. Now, I want you to understand that just because I have realized this and am writing this doesn't mean I have it all figured out. Nor does it mean everything I've waited for has come to pass. I am still waiting. I am still fighting. I still have hard days.

But God's promises stand true. No matter the circumstance, no matter the hard days, no matter what the world throws our way, God is still God and he is still sovereign. When we choose to trust him, we don't have to understand it all. Trust the wait. It will be worth it.

So how can we wait well? Waiting well means hoping for the future God promises while still being faithful in the season we're in. What we learn and how we grow in the waiting are crucial to God's plans for us down the road. Each challenge we face in this season prepares us for the harder challenges that will arise in our future seasons. I know that doesn't sound encouraging and pretty—but it is the cold, hard truth. Try not to fixate on wanting out of your current circumstances, and ask yourself an important question: "What can I learn here that I can use later?" **Don't neglect where you currently are just because it isn't where you expected to be.**

Maybe you've been waiting for healing for years. Maybe you've been waiting to get pregnant—it comes so easily to everyone around you, yet it seems impossible for you. Maybe you're waiting on that forever person to do life with and you are tired of being alone. Maybe you're waiting for a job that doesn't suck the life out of you and you're desperate for one that gives you purpose. I know waiting can be frustrating. It can be exhausting. But perhaps God wants to begin something in you while you wait.

In the waiting, every moment counts. Here are three encouragements for your private times of waiting:

1. Wait intentionally. Take advantage of every moment of this season to grow and learn. This is a time to become the best you that you can be! Read as many books as you can, watch as many sermons as you can, and study Scripture.

2. Wait actively. Waiting doesn't mean sitting around on the sidelines and waiting for your name to be called to enter the big game. There's too much to get done! During this time you can still pursue, honor, and steward what God has already entrusted to you. Serve at your local church or at a worthy cause, meet people for coffee to talk about God's love and goodness, and pursue the dreams God has for you.

3. Wait prayerfully. Some days you will wonder if all the hard work you are doing is for nothing or if God even sees you. Sometimes you will feel forgotten and passed over. Waiting seasons often come with hiddenness and loneliness. Yet keep pressing in, and use this time to draw close to God. Use it to build your prayer life. Pray with fervency and faith!

God wants to do his work in you. He is cultivating within you the strength, character, spirit, and courage to be a great woman of God. And one day, when the time is right, this growth will burst forth and be beautiful—greater than you ever imagined. So don't resent the seasons of waiting; the person you become will be well worth the wait!

Prepared through Pain

"No pain, no gain." Usually we link this phrase to sports. In sports, we can accept that there might be some physical pain along the way as we go after our goal to win games. So how come when it comes to life, as soon as pain hits us, we run, we hide, we become angry, we ignore it, or we become crippled and defined by it? I hope you are beginning to see that pain is not your enemy but your friend. It is not a friend you should invite to live with you—more like the kind of friend who is in your life for a season, needing to teach you something about yourself. Pain may be temporary, but your response to it has long-lasting effects.

People often say, "Ugh, I want more strength," or "I want more endurance," but many don't see that pain is often what provides the opportunity for strength and endurance to grow. Pain can serve you instead of hindering you if only you choose to utilize it. Let's choose together to grow and turn our pain into purpose and power.

> Pain may be temporary, but your response to it has long-lasting effects.

It was a Sunday morning, and I was driving home from church. I answered a call from one of my friends, and she shared news I never thought I would hear. I hung up the phone and immediately pulled over to the side of the road. I was terrified by the hurt that rose up within me. I was shaking and crying, asking God, "Why?" I had never felt weaker and more vulnerable. See, I had never let someone in close enough to be able to hurt me, and as soon as I did, I faced what I feared all along. A battle raged in my head and heart and left me feeling "weak"—a feeling I hated more than anything and had run from for so long. I had always avoided opportunities and relationships to make sure I never felt this way.

Has there ever been someone or something that has emptied you, leaving you without breath or energy to fight? Maybe you normally cover up your reaction or put on a face—you're the one everyone is leaning on and turning to. But this heart-crushing news changes everything.

Let me rewind to tell more of the story that led to this particular moment.

I was the girl who always put on a face of strength and had it all together—nothing phased me. I never let people into the most vulnerable places of my heart because I was afraid of losing what I took pride in—my strength and being in control. For the longest time, I couldn't open up and be vulnerable with people. I couldn't stay in a relationship because I was too afraid of what would happen if I fell for that person. I would lose too much control. Then on one cold, bright day in December, that all changed.

I met someone who invited me into his world and wanted to be a part of mine. From the first date we went on, I knew there was something different and intriguing about him, and I wanted to find out more. On our first date he challenged me with three questions: What is your daily walk with the Lord like and what are you doing to grow it? And what do you want from me? I was so taken aback by his confidence and assertiveness. A few months later we started dating. I felt emotions I never thought I would feel, but every time I felt them, I drew back even more, in fear of the unknown.

One day I was helping him with something around his house because he had torn his ACL and couldn't walk. I looked in the fridge to grab a drink and ran to him, screaming, "I love Cherry Coke!" He laughed and responded, "I love *you*." I looked at him with confusion and fear—we had been dating only a month or two. He started the whole awkward mumbling thing (what you do when you're nervous and don't know what to say): "Umm, I mean, umm, you know, I love Cherry Coke too." Most girls would have been thrilled. Most girls would have screamed and smiled and jumped up and down and said, "I love you too!" Not me. I said, "Okay, see you later, bye!" and walked out and pretended it didn't happen. He later told me he was so upset at himself, he punched his pillow, and blamed the unplanned outburst on being a little out of it after his ACL surgery.

But one evening, a couple of weeks later, I couldn't escape when he sat me down and spoke those three big words yet again but this time with a serious look on his face: "Madison, I love you." Even though I knew I loved this guy, I was terrified to admit it. I had never felt this way before. I felt incredible love growing inside me, but I also still struggled with fear and control. I didn't know how to respond. This time he meant it with all his heart, and I couldn't just walk out. So I looked away for a few moments and then glanced at him with a wry smile and replied, "Thanks," and gave him a pat on the back. I knew that probably wasn't the response he was looking for and was most likely a shot to his pride, but it was easier just to let him love me. That way I wouldn't lose anything.

This continued for months. After a few months had passed, while stargazing at the beach one night, I looked at him with tears in my eyes and said, "I love you too." It caught him off guard, but it was music to his ears as he had been waiting so long to hear those words from me. I was so scared to admit what I already knew and had been running from for months. Fast-forward—we dated for four years, and during that time I learned how to truly love someone with the type of love that isn't based on performance or convenience or whether I was "feeling" it or not. One night I woke up from a dream with a feeling deep within me: "This guy could be my husband!"

We started to discuss rings and venues and our bridal party! I dreamed about it all: the proposal, the wedding, the life together. It consumed me—it was all I could think about! It was my senior year of college, and everyone was getting engaged. Where was my proposal? Where was my ring? I didn't realize it then, but the relationship had become an idol to me.

Everything was great until one day. I don't know how to explain it other than I felt a restlessness and lack of peace in my heart about the relationship. I began to pray about it. I felt God was trying to show me he had a different plan for both of us.

I called my boyfriend over, and after having a conversation, we both agreed ending the relationship would be best. For three days I didn't leave my house, and my eyes were swollen shut from all the tears. I sat and cried for hours, wondering why I had to let go of someone who meant so much to me.

A week passed, and I picked up my phone to call my ex. For the past four years, I had never gone this long without talking to him, and it was killing me. I wanted to know what he was thinking about, what he was doing, and if he was struggling as much as I was. But as I started to make the call, I felt that uneasiness again. So I put the phone down, and I prayed, "Okay, God, I give our relationship to you. It's yours."

A few long and hard months later, I got a phone call—*the* phone call—the kind of phone call that requires you to pull over to the side of the road because you no longer trust your ability to drive. My best friend called me and told me that my ex had started dating someone. What a sting. So fast. So soon. Was I that easy to get over? Did he ever even love me? Many thoughts ran through my mind.

Then she told me *who* he started dating. That was when I had to pull the car over. This couldn't be right. I responded, "Wait, are you sure?" She hesitated but ensured me, "I'm so sorry, Madi. Yes, he is dating *her*." *Her* was one of my close friends from college. I was heartbroken. I was confused.

Deep down I knew they were perfect for each other, and I was happy for them. But I still struggled with the pain and hurt in my heart. I prayed with hot tears, "God, how come I have to go through this season of pain and loneliness, while everyone else can easily and happily move on? God, I don't understand!"

My heart hurt so bad for a long time. Day after day I would go back to my apartment and sit in my room alone, trying my best to cheer on all my other friends in their seasons of happiness and marriage. I hated how weak it made me feel and that there was nothing I could do about it. I was angry because I felt like I got the short end of the stick. I felt like I was the one being punished. But I kept pressing in and trusting. Some days were much harder than others. There were a lot of tears, Nicholas Sparks movies, ice cream, prayer, and journaling.

What does all this have to do with being ready for your moment? I tell you about this season of heartbreak because it was one of the most painful times in my life, and I had no idea what God was up to. I surely could not have foreseen that I would be where I am now. During that season, God used my pain and brokenness, my loneliness and hurt, to develop me, and he armed me with strength and courage to equip me for what was to come. Little did I know that I was being prepared for a time when my pain and brokenness would be on display for all to see.

Sometimes it is through pain and suffering that courage and strength are found, produced, and built. If I hadn't walked through this season of heartbreak, pain, and loneliness, I would not have been prepared or courageous enough to stand firm under pressure with the whole world watching. Sharing this part of my past isn't easy, but I do because I hope my struggle, my pain, and my journey help you find what I found: the courage to embrace who you are, holding firm to your identity in Christ with strength, grace, and confidence. When I was struggling in those painful and heartbroken seasons, I wished I had someone to help me through, someone who would share what got them through their tough times.

When I think about the difficulties I've experienced and the seasons when I felt so much brokenness and loneliness, I realize it was hard to see the potential and have hope for what was to come. I was still grieving over what was lost. But as I reflect back on those times now, I am grateful for the losses and the pain that came with them. I know that is a big statement to make because when you're in the middle of that pain, gratitude is the opposite of what you feel. But I have learned to see the losses and the pain as necessary for what is to come. God had to strengthen me so I would be prepared and tough enough to step into my destiny.

Strength isn't a personality trait or a passed-down blessing from your family. Strength isn't a feeling. Strength isn't built from being perfect and having everything all figured out. And being strong doesn't mean you have no weaknesses or weak moments. All of us have the same opportunity to walk in strength and courage. So why do some do it, and others don't?

Where do I find this "strength"? We find the answer in God's Word. Ephesians 3:16 says, "I pray that out of his glorious riches he may strengthen you with power through his Spirit in your inner being." This means strength comes from the Spirit within us. This verse tells us that we are strong in God. Because he is strong, we can stand strong. This is encouraging because it means we don't have to muster up that strength and courage on our own, hoping we have what it takes to keep going. When we choose to follow Jesus and give him our whole heart, we become one with him—body, soul, and spirit. When you pursue that relationship, the Spirit inside you will continue to show you the way, convict your heart, and give you all you need to be who God has called you to be. The Spirit gives you the discipline you need for the small day-to-day moments and the strength and wisdom you need for the big moments. We still have some work to do and need to take some steps to be prepared, but be encouraged: **the strength to overcome isn't from you or by you, but rather comes from God's Spirit inside you.**

In the seasons of wondering where God is, in the moments unseen by the outside world, there may be times that seem long, painful, and unfair, times when you feel like you can't take another step. I've learned that these are the very times that God uses to protect you and prepare you. God is for you, not against you, and he's got it all under control. Christine Caine encourages us with her words, "Jesus walks on the very waves we think will drown us."[1] He's using these trials to get you in position for the amazing times that are to come. I know this now more than ever. And if I could, I'd go back and tell the Madi answering a call from Los Angeles in the Chick-fil-A drive-through that she was way more ready for the road ahead than she ever knew.

Challenges on Being Ready

1. Shift your perspective. We sometimes fall into the trap of believing that seasons of waiting are lost time. Shift your perspective to see seasons of waiting as preparation for all that God has in store for you. If you are waiting, that means you have something worth waiting for. And trust me when I say that it will be well worth the wait. Whether you are waiting for acceptance into the school of your dreams, a callback, a boyfriend, a job, a gig, or a text back, don't let the waiting consume you. Easier said than done, I know. But hear me when I say that what you are waiting for does not define you.

2. Accept the pain. Pain is not your enemy but a wise teacher. Pain produces perseverance, strength, and grit, and it brings us to our knees and shows us how to trust and surrender. Pain and purpose go hand in hand. We often have a tendency to hide our pain, but when we are open about it with ourselves and those we trust, we may begin to realize the purpose in our pain.

3. Ask for strength to grow. Growth is uncomfortable but necessary. Growth never comes in the form of familiarity and comfort. To grow, you need to recognize what hinders your growth. Ask God to reveal anything in your life that hinders you from living your purpose.

Many people will never reach their full potential because they aren't willing to brave the messy and painful moments. Yet it is often the pain, the unknown, the shaky "Okay, Lord, your will be done!" moments that take you to places you never thought you could go. Allow God to develop you and you will be amazed at what he can do through you. Don't be afraid of the preparation, for it always precedes the promise.

CHAPTER 3

THE POWER OF THE PRESEASON

Training for Your Big Moment in Everyday Moments

I had been in the Bachelor mansion only a few days, and I was already beginning to ask the question: What have I gotten myself into? We hadn't been filming long, but already, it had been late nights, early mornings, a lot of interviews, and a lot of drama.

For those of you who have never watched *The Bachelor*, each episode features a series of dates that different contestants are invited on. Around the same time each day, usually midmorning, everyone gathers in the living room for the reading of the date card. The date card is a basic white card inside an envelope containing the names of the girls (or girl) who get to go on a date with the Bachelor. The moment is usually filled with anticipation as each girl hopes her name will be called. There are three date cards each week. The first two weeks of the show, the date cards consist of two group dates and one lucky girl's one-on-one date.

As all the girls sat down on the big comfy sofa, already feeling like forever friends, we all cuddled up next to each other and anxiously waited for *the* knock. As soon as the knock came, one of the contestants went to the door to receive the date card. I had my fingers crossed, hoping my name would be called for the first one-on-one date. Even though getting the first date would be great, it would also come with a lot of pressure.

I am sure I looked shocked when I heard my name called. Before I had time to process what was happening, there was another knock on the door. I was told to go answer. I opened the door, and there was a package with my name on it. Inside the beautifully wrapped package was a pink dress and a pair of high heels. Immediately we all tried to guess what the date could be. The date card read, "Madison, I want to show you what forever could look like." I couldn't believe the Bachelor had picked me for the first one-on-one date of the season!

I went upstairs to get ready for my date. I started to get nervous. "Am I prepared for this? What if I don't get a rose? What if I don't like him? What if he doesn't like me?" Part of my nerves were because none of us girls knew much about Peter since this was the first date. It helped that the dress fit like a glove. After I got ready, I sat and waited for Peter to arrive. I wondered, "Am I prepared? What am I doing here? What will we even talk about?"

Peter finally arrived and we headed to the car. He wouldn't tell me where we were going, but he seemed much more nervous than I was. His palms were sweaty, his knees were shaking, and he was sweating through his shirt. I finally looked at him and said, "You are way more nervous than me. Are you okay?" We pulled up to a house and walked through the gate, where we found about fifty people dressed up and sitting in fancy white chairs. At first I thought, "Is this guy trying to marry me already?" I knew that couldn't be right. Moments later, when the music started playing and Peter took his spot on the stage, I understood why we were there. His parents were renewing their vows! Now I understood why he had been so nervous. My heart leaped; I felt honored to be a part of such a special day.

The setup was beautiful. Peter's parents stood under a flowered arch in the backyard of their home and exchanged the same vows they had decades before. There were many tears and many cheers and a whole lot of yummy food! It couldn't have been a better first date—although I was continually distracted by how bad my feet were hurting me in those heels. As soon as I could, I ripped off my shoes and walked around barefoot. I thought, "Now I'm ready to dance!" Peter taught me a few swing-dance moves, so I was ready to teach him a few of mine. I asked the DJ to play "Teach Me How to Dougie," my go-to dance, and I started breaking it down, showing Peter and his family how to dougie. Peter attempted but failed miserably. I laughed so hard my stomach hurt. It was a special day of meeting his closest friends and family and seeing what a future would be like with him.

The day ended and I left to go back to my hotel room to get dressed for the evening portion of the date, when it would be just the two of us. I took a nap and soaked my feet in warm water since they hurt so bad from the high heels. Finally, some alone time! I took time to pray and journal, for I knew the conversation with Peter that night would be much deeper than the casual, fun, small talk we'd had so far. My thoughts swirled inside my head as I wondered where the conversation would go. "Will he ask me about my family? My faith? My past relationships?" I sat with my feet in the tub, playing through every scenario in my mind. I prayed one last prayer, "Okay,

Lord, it's in your hands!" I closed my journal, drained the bath, and wiped off my sore and throbbing feet.

I picked out one of my favorite jumpsuits for the evening. Jumpsuits were my thing! I wasn't a huge fan of dresses. When I showed up to the dinner date, my mouth dropped at what I saw. It was a massive oak tree with strings of lights dangling from the branches. It was dark out, and the stars were already shining bright. A perfect little two-person table sat right under the big oak tree. For me, it was the definition of a perfect date night.

We sat and talked about how much fun we had seeing his family and friends earlier that day. I then opened up and shared with him how much family means to me and my expectations regarding relationships and marriage. We connected much better than I thought we would, and opening up to him was so easy. We had great conversation, and our relationship was already beginning to feel so real that I forgot I was even on TV! That is, until Peter paused and grabbed the rose sitting on the table and asked me, "Madison, will you accept this rose?" Of course I accepted! For this was the golden ticket! I was asked on the first one-on-one date and got the rose. For those of you who have never seen the show, the rose signified that the Bachelor liked you and would like to keep you around for another week until the next rose handout moment! Each week there would be rose ceremonies held, and the girls who didn't get roses would be sent home. I didn't know what this journey had in store for me, but, hey, this week, I got my rose!

Could this night get any better? We started walking and he told me he had a surprise for me. We entered a barn and flowers were everywhere. Music artist Tenille Arts was on the stage. A private concert—what a fairy tale! As we danced, I couldn't believe I had just met this guy. I felt like I had known him for a long time. In the middle of the song, a group of people rushed in. At first I thought they were backup dancers. I thought, "This is kind of weird, but I'll go with it!" As they came closer, I noticed it was Peter's friends and family. We had so much fun dancing and singing. I didn't want the night to end. But I knew it had to, and I had to deal with the harsh reality: I wasn't the only girl.

When I got back to the mansion and reflected and journaled about my date with Peter, I realized I was ready for this. I was prepared. I didn't know what the journey would look like, but I knew I was supposed to be here to find out. I was ready because I had prepared well. When the cameras were on me, I didn't feel the need to put on a show or give the perfect answer or know just what to say or do. I didn't feel pressure to change who I was to be accepted or loved by others. I was able to be fully myself. In these moments, with all eyes on me, I knew that my truest, inner self is what was on display.

Let's get one thing straight: I am not perfect by any means. I have had many moments when I allowed my environment to shape me or change me, moments when I didn't stay true to myself and my convictions. Yet along the way, through some failure and resistance, I grew in courage and confidence. I have learned that I am able to stand firm in my convictions and stay true to myself not because I am strong in a moment of pressure but because I was strong in the moments of preparation.

Now, I understand that your moments of preparation or pressure might not look like mine, nor should they. I don't foresee all of you stepping into the unknown of reality TV. I share with you my story and what I've learned along the way, but it is important to note that not all my moments of pressure were on display for millions to see. I have fought and will have to continue to fight day-to-day pressures and temptations. I want you to understand the message here: **It's not about what your big moment looks like; it's about what your small moments consistently look like.**

One of your big moments may be when you are with a group of friends and they are bullying some girl because of how she looks. How will you respond? Will you join in? Will you sit back and remain silent? Will you hope someone else has the courage to defend her? It's the smaller moments—the preparation, the day-to-day choices and decisions—that will prepare you to stand up for that girl.

> Your desired future will arrive only at the level of your preparation for it.

Your desired future will arrive only at the level of your preparation for it. Without preparation, you won't be able to withstand the pressures. You won't be able to overcome the temptations.

To stand firm in strength and conviction doesn't mean every moment comes with ease and convenience. Some moments catch you off guard and you get your feet kicked out from under you. Sometimes you won't want to stand firm or won't feel much courage in the moment. Preparation acts as the backbone to true godly courage and strength. Preparation gives you what you need to stand firm in whatever is handed to you.

Preseason

Most people know one thing about my family and me: we are a basketball family. Sports have always been a big part of our world, especially basketball. My dad coached basketball, so it was inevitable that his daughters would play. My two sisters, Mallory and Mary Mykal, and I didn't grow up camping, skiing, deep-sea fishing, skating, crafting, or whatever else seemed to be the "thing to do"; we grew up in the gym. We probably spent more time in the gym than anywhere else. My dad was my coach for most of my basketball career, and, yes, I could tell you plenty of stories, but what I want to highlight here is that sports have shaped a big part of who I am. But there were many moments in playing sports that weren't always enjoyable during the process.

I always dreaded one thing about sports: preseason. My dad would use preseason to get our team ready for the upcoming season. Our preseason seemed to start earlier each year and become harder and harder. The word *preseason* still makes me break out in a cold sweat. It was always a time of breaking down and rebuilding. It was a time when my body had to get back into shape so that when the season came, I would be ready for the long and tough games. It was the hardest thing my body ever had to do. Preseason was harder than any game ever was.

My dad coached boys and girls basketball and didn't believe in having separate preseasons. The girls were forced to scrimmage against the guys. Imagine how awkward it would be to guard the boy you like on the court. Yeah, I had to do this. Most guys were terrified even to talk to me because my dad was their coach. Every once in a while, there would be a few brave souls. So when I did have a crush on one of my dad's players, I would have to scrimmage against him! Let's just say beating your crush one-on-one makes it a little awkward.

I can still envision the locker room after each preseason practice. Usually girls were throwing up, sitting in ice baths, or lying on the floor trying to catch their breath. Unfortunately, many of my teammates played other sports that kept them from being able to come to preseason. Not me, of course—my dad wouldn't let me miss a day of preseason if my life depended on it.

Most days consisted of running hills, jumping rope, scrimmaging against the guys, and doing exercises such as pyramids, push-ups, four-minute drills, and one-mile runs, followed by ice baths, IcyHot, and Advil. My dad enjoyed pushing us past our breaking points. He liked the preseason process, I would like to say, a little too much. He always believed greatness was achieved in the off-season and the day-to-day grind, not in the games, when the crowd was there to watch and cheer us on. Dad would come up with drills that would challenge our skills, our attitude, our strength, and our endurance. He had one drill where he would throw up the ball, call up two people to stand at the free-throw line, and attempt to hit the rim—purposefully missing. The first person to grab the rebound and score would win. Each time we lost, an extra down-and-back was added to our running after practice. People would almost kill each other trying to get the rebound and put back. But that didn't stop me from going after the ball and doing what it took to win.

God gets us ready in the same way, but thankfully not through long hours of physical training. Preseason isn't fun, but it's needed if you are going to be all God has called you to be.

How can you prepare in your preseason? You have to have a goal that pushes you because staying in your comfort zone is never adequate preparation. In basketball, the goal of preseason was to make it gradually harder each week. My dad knew we couldn't get season-ready overnight; our bodies wouldn't be ready for that. Certain steps of preparation were required, and there was no room for shortcuts. Our muscles had to be built up incrementally, through practice, through putting in the time and sweat and work every day. Preseason can be a long process, but it always pays off during games. My dad told me that when he would watch our team or other teams play, he could always spot the players who took preseason seriously versus the ones who didn't show up or just went through the motions. **Preparation can be painful, just like preseason, but it will be what sets you apart from everyone else.**

I hated preseason. But it was always the most critical time, affecting every part of my game and whether I improved or not. In preseason I would push my body to limits I didn't even know existed, squeezing every last drop of energy out of myself. Some mornings I would wake up feeling like I had been hit by a train, but day after day I improved. I trained harder. I became stronger, more resilient, more prepared. When the season came, I was ready.

Don't Despise Small Beginnings

Have you ever been snow skiing? If so, do you remember your first time? I do. It was quite the painful experience. I was twenty years old and was on vacation with my boyfriend and his family in Colorado. I had never been skiing before, but I thought it would be fun. Oh, did I mention this was the first time I had met his whole family? We all put on our ski suits. Everyone headed up to the ski lift and waited to be dropped off at what they call a black diamond ski run. Not me, I was getting ready to be dropped off on the bunny slope. Because it was my first time skiing, I was told I had to sign up for ski school.

I thought, "Hey, I'm an athlete, so this will be easy." I was dead wrong. My ski class was filled with little kids. I was the only one over the age of ten. Yet I was the worst one in the class. I was horrible, and I hate not being good at things, especially when I am trying to impress a guy I like. My boyfriend was off to the side watching me as I fell on my face time after time, while he did flips and twists and turns and showed off his sick tricks. The more frustrated I became, the worse I got. I became so angry that I couldn't stop without falling and that I couldn't do all the cool tricks he and his family could do.

45

As the day went on, I got a little better but still couldn't figure out how to slow down. One time going down the bunny slope, I went really fast and couldn't seem to stop. The next thing I knew, I had taken out my seventy-something-year-old instructor. My skis had gone everywhere, and all the kids in my class stared and laughed at me. Thankfully, the instructor was okay. But I looked up and there was my boyfriend laughing and videotaping me. My instructor might have been fine, but my pride was not.

I asked my boyfriend if I could go on the black diamond. I insisted that I was ready. He looked at me like I was crazy and replied, "Do you not remember the tumble you just had a few moments ago? Let's try again tomorrow." I was so mad. I didn't want to stay on the bunny slopes anymore. That was for little kids! He continued to explain that the black diamond slope is dangerous if you aren't prepared to navigate it. He explained that the slopes were massive and had many trees, cliffs, and rocky areas and that sometimes even those who have trained and prepared well get hurt on these slopes.

I understood what he was saying and that he was trying to look out for me, but I was still mad and gave him the silent treatment the rest of the day. Real mature, I know. Later that night I realized the weight of his words. The black diamond slope, which is fun and exciting and packed with thrill and adventure, is where everyone seeks to be, where all the Instagrammable photos are taken, but can also be dangerous if one isn't properly prepared. The same goes for life. Most people don't enjoy training and preparing on the bunny slopes. Those aren't the pictures that are posted or the stories that are told. Yet the black diamond is possible to attain only if one prepares on the bunny slope. Aiming for the heights before you're ready can be disastrous. Getting a husband, a job, a platform, an opportunity, or a promotion before you're ready can be dangerous.

What I learned through seasons of nos, closed doors, waiting, and painful moments was that preparation precedes opportunity. You don't deserve the platform, the job, or the husband if you aren't willing to go through the process to be able to handle it. I learned not to despise the little lessons that are to be learned along the way.

Zechariah 4:10 (NLT) says, "Do not despise these small beginnings, for the LORD rejoices to see the work begin." This verse continues to challenge me. It's easy to want only the big moments, especially in our day and age. Everyone seems to want overnight fame, instant likes, immediate gratification, big events and parties, and the moments that make them the hero. Even though many of us desire some of these things, most of us aren't willing to put in the work to prepare by treating every moment and task like it matters. **The smaller moments that nobody sees or deems important make the biggest difference.** The moments of making your bed every morning, saying hi to a stranger, choosing an apple over a cookie, spending ten minutes every day in God's Word, writing a school paper with excellence, getting up early to exercise, making dinner for your husband, praying over your family, choosing to stay in instead of go out, paying for a meal for the car behind you, reading a chapter of a book—these are the moments that shape you, refine you, and prepare you for the bigger moments.

> Preparation precedes opportunity.

The small moments are your training ground, your preseason, for the big moments.

We have more days of normalcy than we do spectacular and life-changing days. That's why the little moments matter. Moment-makers do the little things with excellence and care.

We have to practice doing the small things well. What you practice—the daily choices and habits that you build and make—becomes permanent. It's like a basketball player who doesn't leave the gym before he shoots one hundred free throws. Day after day, it seems like a mundane or small task. But that repeated motion over time becomes muscle memory. The player could close his eyes and still be able to make that free throw. Many players might see it as insignificant. It's just a free throw. They may ask themselves, "Why is he wasting his time shooting all those free throws?" Yet when it's the championship game, a foul is called, the game is on the line, and one free throw is all the team needs to win, I can guarantee you, they are going to want homeboy, who spent hours every day shooting free throws, on the line to secure the win. What you practice becomes your permanent reality. If you want to win the game, you have to be willing to put in the hours and make the tough decisions and sacrifices.

Those who want to be great at something are willing to put in the time to practice and become the best. My dad would always quote James Baker: "Prior preparation prevents poor performance."[1] Try saying that five times—ha! But think about it: even Michael Jordan, after winning a national title, would go back to the gym the next day to keep practicing to get better. You know where Michael Phelps went after he took home the gold medal? Back to the pool to practice and prepare for the next match. We are always practicing something. Are you learning to trust the process of preparation? Are you practicing good habits?

If you are always preparing for something, what are you preparing for?

Preparing for Your Moment: A Practical Plan

Often we let life come at us, and we figure it out as we go. Meanwhile, we fantasize about getting our "big break," as if when a big opportunity comes knocking, *then* we'll take it and run with it. But would we? If we live our lives on autopilot, passively responding and reacting to events that come our way, will a big moment be enough to flip the switch and stir us into action? Moments large and small *do* come our way in life, but sadly many of us aren't ready for them.

I don't want that to be the case for you and me. There is too much greatness inside you to allow the things of the world just to "happen" to you or define you. And the big moments matter too much to let our fate be decided on a whim.

I'm thinking about the milestone moments—big, amazing, life-changing moments:

the moment you're offered the job that could change your career and life forever

the moment you're told those two big words—*you're pregnant*—after trying for years

the moment you finally finish that book or song or film you've been working on for what seems like forever

the moment you graduate school after years of dedication and financial struggles

the moment you knock down the shot to win the game for your team after months of training

the moment you say "I do" after years of waiting and praying

the moment you have an opportunity in your job or field to do something that has never been done before

I'm also thinking about the moments of pressure or pain that will challenge you to your core, the moments that surprise you and hurt you so deeply that you don't know if you will be able to go on.

the moment someone took your innocence away from you

the moment you are told by the doctor, "There is nothing else
we can do."

the moment you lose someone you care about

the moment someone offers you drugs for the first time

the moment the boy tells you, "If you do this, I will
love you."

the moment a bully tells you to kill yourself because "no one
likes you"

the moment when the only out looks like pills, alcohol, or
a gun

How do we handle these moments? How do we respond? How can we be prepared? Let's talk practically.

Predecide Who You Want to Be

First, we should predecide what we are going to do before the situation ever arises. I have made it a discipline to try not to make a big decision in the heat of the moment. We often agonize over non-critical decisions. Deciding what kind of purse to buy is probably not going to have a big impact on our future. Deciding how to style our hair most likely isn't going to impact our closest relationships. We think long and hard about the material decisions. Yet when it comes to the important behavioral decisions, which are far more crucial to our destiny, people often just react.

Why decide in the moment when you can decide in advance? Professional athletes do it. Airline pilots do it. Musicians do it. The most successful people decide their game plan beforehand. If we took time to reflect on the decisions we need to make, I wonder how many of them we could predecide. Of course there are some things we can never predict. But through seasons of preparation and reflection, we ready ourselves to make the best decisions possible when the moments of pressure hit.

Also, it helps to tell others about your predecisions. Once someone knows about a decision or dream you have, you automatically become more motivated to achieve it. There is power in accountability. I have three people I tell my predecisions to. Those three people hold me accountable and challenge me to stick to those commitments.

Practice Doing Small Things Well

Being faithful with small things will prepare you to be faithful with more. To be your best *then*, you must be your best now. Practice, practice, practice. Hard work is the key to success. You can always improve, and practice makes permanent! The more effort you put in, the more you get out.

Remember, you have to master the bunny slopes before the black diamonds!

Trust the Process

Third, it is important to understand that preparation is a process. It isn't immediate. It takes time. You have to be willing to put in the time and effort to get the results you are looking for. Do the small things well and be consistent. Don't rush the preparation process or resent it. There is a lot to learn and experience through it. It's not always fun, easy, or glamorous. The process and journey can be long and painful. But even the best and most elaborate meals take the longest to prepare—how much more, then, should we?

Commit to Growing

Every one of us will have many life-defining moments. Yet if we approach a big moment with the mindset of, "I have only one shot. This is make-or-break," we are bound to choke. The first step to preparing yourself for a life-defining moment is to understand that failing or losing at any one moment does not mean game over. Life is a sum total of a bunch of moments; it's what we do with those moments that matter. We have to realize that the *small* moments matter just as much as, if not more, than a life-defining moment. Through the day-to-day we are learning, preparing, and growing. We should not resent or run from the past or be too busy planning our future. **We are called to be fully present in the now, and that is how we will be prepared for the important moments to come.**

Prepare to Make Sacrifices

There will be times when you have to sacrifice expectations and comfort to step into all that God has for you. Often preparation is uncomfortable, unfamiliar, even painful. But without it, you wouldn't be all that God wants you to be or be ready to do all that God has called you to do.

A great moment, a moment of impact and significance, isn't born in the spotlight; it's born before the moment ever arrives. **What happens before that moment is what makes it great.** Those moments when we live out the everyday, *small* tasks of our lives shape and prepare us for the bigger moments that we desire. Every hard decision we've had to make, all the private battles we've had to fight, every small and big experience we've had has prepared us for such a moment as this.

Challenges on Preparation

1. Anchor yourself in a vision of who you want to be. If you don't know *why* you're doing what you're doing, you'll be inconsistent. You have to ask, "What kind of person do I want to be? What kind of life do I want to live?" Don't let other people make those decisions for you. Decide right now, and let that be your why—the purpose behind every decision you make.

2. Commit to your preseason. Practice rarely makes perfect, but it *will* strengthen the muscles you need most for game time. Your dream for your future depends on what you are doing today. The day-to-day practices of discipline and intentionality will dictate when or if you ever reach your long-term dream. *You will play how you practice.*

3. What is inside of you is what will come out of you. So what you allow in, who you invite in, and what you feed yourself matters! Make sure that you are investing wisely. You will be able to stand firm under pressure because you invested in yourself and prepared well.

CHAPTER 4

SAY GOODBYE TO THE SNOOZE BUTTON

Choosing Discipline Even When It's Difficult

You snooze you lose!

Are there any phrases or words that send chills down your back and make you instantly irritated? This is mine. I don't like to lose, but I do like to snooze, and this time it bit me in the butt. It was my first semester of college. I was loving all the freedom and down-time. It was amazing! But I didn't realize how hard staying disciplined would be. I didn't have my parents to remind me about my homework or to wake me up for class—I was all I had.

One night I stayed up late to study. I had my routine down: chocolate milk and flash cards. Don't ask me why, but it worked every time. The chocolate milk was my treat and also gave me energy to study. I finished studying around midnight and set my alarm to wake up early so I could go back over the information before my test the next morning at 8:00 a.m. When I woke up, I rolled over and looked at the clock: 10:30 a.m. What! How did I not wake up? I panicked. What was I going to do? I quickly dressed and rushed to my teacher's office. Before I could even get a sentence out, she said, "Let me guess: you overslept." I knew this situation could go one of two ways: either she would be a cool teacher and let me sit down and take the test, or she'd be tough and refuse to let me make it up. I explained to her that I had studied hard and knew all the information but just happened to sleep through my alarm. My mom always says I should have been a lawyer because I can usually argue my way out of anything. Not this time. My teacher looked at me and said those horrible words: "You snooze you lose." What a dagger. Getting a zero on a test is almost impossible to recover from, and it was early in the semester. I was going to need perfect scores on all my other work.

I left her office so frustrated. I called her a few names in my head. I kept replaying her "you snooze you lose" remark in a smug, sarcastic tone in my head. I marched back into my room and ripped up all my note cards. All that studying for nothing! I was so upset with the teacher. How could she say that? Then after I calmed down and thought about the situation, I realized she was right. I did lose, and it was because I was snoozing, and those were the facts.

In that moment, I realized I didn't want to fail moving forward in life because of my lack of discipline. I didn't want to be the reason I missed out on opportunities. So I made a decision: no more snoozing and losing. If I failed, it wouldn't be because I didn't show up and give my best. From that point on, I was going to set five alarms on full blast to make sure I got up. I felt sorry for my roommate, but I had to do what I had to do. And it worked.

Throughout the rest of my time in college, I did not once miss another test because I overslept. Thankfully for the rest of that semester, I did well on the remaining assignments and was able to come out with a B. I'll take it! I learned a valuable lesson. I can't blame other people for my mistakes. I can't put my loss on them, when it was I who was the snoozer!

Have you ever hit the snooze button and missed something important? Not being able to take that test taught me a lot. I realized that what feels good in the moment is not always what's best for me in the long run. Hitting that snooze button and ignoring the consequences is a lot easier and feels a lot better. Getting up to study, work, or work out is hard. It would be easier to keep telling ourselves, "I'll start tomorrow," or "Just five more minutes."

Self-discipline isn't fun or easy or convenient, yet it sets apart the good from the great. It is required to be prepared to seize the moments of pressure and opportunity. You will never feel like changing. So stop waiting for a perfect time. You have to force yourself to be uncomfortable. Action leads to motivation. Those first few minutes when you push yourself out of bed early in the morning aren't fun. But the rest of the day is good because you started not with procrastination or laziness but with self-discipline.

What is the first decision you made this morning? Some research says you can tell a lot about a person by what they do first, whether it is the first thing of the day, the month, or the year. It even includes what they do first with their money, time, and so on. What we value most usually gets our "first." My first is set aside for God. In everything that I do, he gets the first of it—the first fifteen minutes of my day, the first day of my week, the first ten percent of my monthly income. My experience is that when you give God the first, he will bless and take care of the rest.

So next time your alarm goes off, toss aside your sheets and blankets, stand up, make your bed, and start your day. No snooze. No lying there for fifteen minutes and scrolling. No debating. Get up and start your day with excellence. Standing strong in moments of pressure starts with daily decisions to be the best you can be and choosing discipline over desire. **Right now you have to do what you don't want to do so that later you can be everything you dreamed you'd be.** You are set apart for this moment in time, but you will need discipline to walk it out.

We all have high hopes and great dreams, but many of us never reach them because we lack discipline. What we do and what we should do don't line up. Self-discipline means putting off your immediate comfort or desires in favor of long-term success. As you continue to discipline yourself, you will achieve more and more in life, be ready for whatever moments come your way, grow your self-confidence, and will find yourself more energized and positive throughout the day. Maybe you are thinking, "Madi, all that sounds good, but how do I become more disciplined? Where do I even start?" We start with taking a hard look at what we prioritize.

Prioritize Values over Feelings

Discipline requires you to place your steadfast values over your fleeting feelings.

I am sure many of us have had moments of giving in to those homemade chocolate chip cookies, or procrastinating our homework because watching TV is more appealing, or hitting the snooze button instead of waking up early and getting our day going. On a deeper level, I am sure many of us have also had moments of going further than we wanted to or giving in to peer pressure because in the moment it felt good or seemed right, but outside the moment it brought resentment and shame. These struggles are not a question to your strength or character; the issue is your lack of discipline. As I've mentioned, it's what you do before the big moment arrives that sets you up for either success or failure.

I have been asked many times, "How do you stay motivated?" or "What keeps you motivated?" I often struggle with a response because the truth is that I'm not always motivated. Crazy, I know.

> Discipline requires you to place your steadfast values over your fleeting feelings.

I too sometimes just want to be lazy or to instantly satisfy my appetite or mood. But I've realized that motivation is a feeling and that it comes and goes (it feels like it does a lot more going than coming!). Feelings are fleeting, meaning they could be here today and gone tomorrow. Feelings are never consistent because they are dictated by many other moving and uncontrollable factors.

So how do I stay motivated? I don't. I stay disciplined. Discipline makes all the difference. It keeps me on track with my goals even when I don't feel like it. It helps me constantly prioritize my values. It gives me the ability to be consistent in whatever I do and to always finish well. It equips me with what I need so that I don't compromise who I am. Discipline is consistently doing small things that eventually turn into reaching the big "far off" goals. Don't get me wrong—motivation is great. A solid playlist can push me through the last stretch of my run, but it won't always get me to the gym. Discipline is necessary for us moment-makers so that when challenges, pressures, or opportunities come, we wake up ready to face our day with excellence!

The first step in developing self-discipline is understanding, as Chris Hodges says, that choices should lead and feelings should follow.[1] Then when temptations approach, you already know how you will respond. It is important that we develop the strength to be able to give up something now to gain something better later. Most people are led by their feelings and desire for instant gratification. This can be dangerous. If we allow our feelings to lead us, down the road we may find ourselves disappointed and regretful of where we are. Your feelings are always valid, but they aren't always right. At least, I know my feelings can be pretty flaky and inconsistent. Can you relate?

Feelings are always valid, but they aren't always right.

You may feel alone, but that does not mean you are alone. You may feel unattractive, but that does not mean others think you're ugly. You may feel life is not worth living, but that does not mean you don't have a purpose on this earth. You may feel rejected, ashamed, or hurt, but that doesn't mean you'll always feel this way. Feelings come and go; they are inconsistent. That's why we can't live our lives based strictly on whatever we feel in the moment. That's why we shouldn't make long-term decisions based on short-term feelings.

Of course, those who tout our cultural mantra of "You only live once" (YOLO) would disagree with me. The YOLO mentality says just do whatever you feel and whatever makes you happy! Whatever feels good in the moment, do it! This is what our culture preaches. I am not here to tell you to ignore your feelings—quite the opposite! Our feelings do matter and often they point toward something much deeper that needs attention. Your feelings are indicators of where you feel lack and where you feel abundance. So take a serious look at your feelings—they are trying to tell you something! But know that feelings are poor decision-makers when such choices come at the expense of facts.

Prioritize Important over Immediate

Discipline requires you to value what is important over what is immediate.

Situations or circumstances you couldn't predict or plan for will always pop up. With everything pulling at our attention, we need to know what we deem as most important. This is the art of prioritizing. Have you ever heard of the rocks and a jar illustration? Well, to sum it up, you have a jar and some big rocks and some small rocks. If you put the small rocks in the jar first, the jar will be unable to fit all the rocks. But if you put the big rocks in first, the small rocks will fall between the cracks and all the rocks will fit in the jar. The same goes for our schedules and time. We have to prioritize what is most important, not what we want in the moment or the urgent things that vie for our attention throughout the day. If we prioritize whatever comes up that day, we won't accomplish what is truly important. That's why it is necessary to have priorities—so you don't become lost in the day-to-day affairs but are instead able to stay focused on your long-term vision or goal.

Let me tell you about a time when my family accidentally lost my little sister at a national championship football game. This is everyone's worst nightmare, right? Thousands of people everywhere. Everyone walking at once, bumping shoulders and yelling. You can't see anything or hear anything. Not to mention we are in a stadium that is unfamiliar to us. My youngest sister, Mary, was six years old at the time. She was a tiny thing. She could've passed for a four-year-old if it weren't for her long, thick hair and sick basketball moves. After the game ended, my family decided to leave quickly so we could go out and celebrate. We hoped to avoid traffic so we could spend more time enjoying our night. We made a group decision to head out.

As we were exiting the stadium, I looked to my mom and said, "Wait, where is Mary?" My mom looked at my dad with fear in her eyes and immediately ran back to our seats. We got to our seats and she was nowhere to be found. My mom started crying and freaking out. My dad tried to calm her down while trying to think about where Mary could possibly have gone. After looking around, we went up to someone who worked at the stadium and explained the situation. He made a few calls on his walkie-talkie, and one of his managers came walking out, holding Mary's little hand. We all ran and grabbed her and embraced her. She looked at my mom and dad with a smile on her face and said, "I wanted to collect more cups." She held up at least six left-behind souvenir cups she had stacked together. She said, "I knew you liked them, Daddy, so I wanted to find you more!"

We asked her what she did when she noticed that we were nowhere to be found, and she said, "I finished picking up my cups, and I went and found a security guard." My parents looked as if they had created baby Einstein. They couldn't believe she handled herself with so much grace, composure, and confidence. That day we learned that Mary was even smarter than we thought. We also learned the hard way to value what is important over what is immediate. We were in such a rush to leave that we left behind what was most important to us. This is a valuable lesson for you and me. There will always be things vying for our time and attention, and it's easy to rush through life looking for the next best thing or following whatever urgencies pop up, yet we need to always look for the important over the immediate.

How can we practically implement this in our lives? I have two suggestions for you. First, create a nonnegotiable schedule for the month, week, and day. A nonnegotiable schedule (NNS) means that certain time slots on that schedule will not change, no matter what comes up. That means if a cute boy asks you to coffee but you haven't accomplished the tasks on your NNS, it's a no go. Now, this can sound a little military-like. I am not telling you not to enjoy your life or not to make the most of the opportunities that come, but make sure you don't compromise or settle for something now that could cost you something later. This unchangeable schedule doesn't have to be crazy intense or unrealistic—in

> Don't compromise or settle for something now that could cost you something later.

fact, it should be the opposite. You should never put too much on your plate, which only sets you up for failure or stretches you too thin; your list should be simple yet strategic.

My daily nonnegotiable schedule looks something like this: make my bed, spend at least fifteen minutes with God every day (five minutes in the Word, five minutes in prayer, and five minutes in worship), do some form of exercise or physical activity, encourage someone, and read a chapter of a book. Now, all of this combined could be done in under an hour. So I want to be clear: Doing more is not always greater, and checking off the boxes of your to-do list does not mean you are productive. I would rather do fewer things and do them well than put a million things on my plate and give only ten percent effort. Every day I remind myself of these five daily activities on my nonnegotiable schedule. As I create my schedule for the day, I make sure to put those five at the top of my list. Although, I'm not always perfect in this department—like when my friends come into town or if I have an unexpected appointment—I continue to strive hard to prioritize what is important and valuable to me over the immediate impulses or distractions.

You can always tell what a person values by how they spend

their time, for time is the most precious thing we have. You can't get it back or buy it back. So use your time wisely. Right now, grab a pen and paper and create your own personal NNS for your week or month. It may seem overwhelming, so start small. Start writing out your day, then your week, then your month. *Discipline* might sound like a daunting word, but once you taste the reward of gaining the important over the immediate, you won't ever want to look back.

Prioritize Right over Easy

Discipline requires you to do the right thing over the easy thing.

Have you ever done something and immediately wished you could take it back? Have you ever reacted out of anger or frustration, then immediately regretted it? I can't tell you how many times I have honked my horn or swerved angrily around a car in front of me only to realize it was a teacher or friend. I can't admit how many times I have reacted with a harsh response because someone said something that hurt me or irritated me, only to realize I was the one who took it the wrong way. In the heat of the moment, it's often hard to do the right thing. After I have made the mistake, it's even harder to go apologize and admit I was wrong.

One instance like this stands out in my memory. I am embarrassed even to share, but hey, let's be real here. As you read in the previous chapter, sports are a big part of my life and my family's world. My dad has coached for Auburn University men's basketball for the past seven years, and a few years ago the team did really well and made it all the way to the Final Four in the March Madness tournament. It had been a crazy season of overcoming all odds to get there, yet we finally made it to the Final Four.

Throughout the game, both teams went back and forth, but the last two minutes of the game Auburn led in points. Just when we thought the game had ended in an Auburn victory, the refs called a foul with .6 seconds left in the game. The player on the other team went up to the free-throw line and made the shots with ease. The clock ran out, and the opposing team won the game by one point.

I can hardly express the anger I felt in that moment. I know it sounds crazy—like, Madi, it was just a basketball game. But if you haven't picked up on this by now, I am extremely competitive. As my mom and my sisters and I walked outside, we ran into a group of the other team's fans. They were taunting us and stood in front of us chanting their school anthem. I finally had all I could take, so I turned to them, locked eyes with them and screamed at the top of my lungs our school's war cry, "*War Eagle!*" Wide-eyed, they stared, not expecting that kind of a reaction to come out of me.

I guess my reaction did enough to send them away, but my mom's and sisters' faces looked distraught, like I had committed a crime. They still joke about that moment and how I let my frustration get the best of me. As I reflect on that situation, I am embarrassed that I reacted that way. The valuable lesson I learned: doing the right thing is not always easy, especially in the heat of the moment. I should have apologized to those fans.

In the moment after the basketball game, I let my feelings lead me, and I did the easy thing: I reacted. But sometimes it isn't only emotions that keep me from doing the right thing; sometimes it's laziness, pride, or fear of what other people will think. Throughout high school and my first semester of college, I often feared doing what was right because I worried that I would lose my friendships or that I would be judged. There were even times on *The Bachelor* when I worried whether doing the right thing would come with a heavy cost.

Maybe you struggle to consistently choose the right thing over the easy thing in the day-to-day activities like making your bed, spending quality time with God, picking up trash when you see it, or encouraging someone each day. Maybe you find yourself constantly surrounded by compromising situations, like cheating on a test, giving in to peer or relationship pressure, or reacting with frustration instead of responding with grace and understanding. There are many situations in which doing the right thing seems hard, impossible, or lonely. Sometimes doing the right thing can come with attacks or consequences. Sometimes it comes with getting mocked and laughed at or judged by people who don't live with the same conviction and understanding.

> Doing what is easy is rarely right, and doing what is right is rarely easy.

Much of the time doing the right thing will go against our natural feelings and impulsive emotions. I guarantee you this: doing what is easy is rarely right, and doing what is right is rarely easy. But it will always be worth it. Discipline requires us to prioritize and choose right over easy.

So let's talk about some practical ways to prioritize what's right over what's easy. How do we walk out that decision? We must learn to be brave in our beliefs, consistent with convictions and commitments, and humble in our hearts.

Deciding to do the right thing when everyone else is doing the easy thing is incredibly difficult. To do what you feel is right, you have to be brave and risk looking like the oddball, weirdo, or prude. Being brave in the moment sucks, but you will have more inner peace and, if others are watching, will inspire and encourage others along the way.

When disciplining yourself to choose right over easy, you have to be consistent. This is possibly one of the hardest steps in developing self-discipline. Starting something is easy, but finishing it is hard. Think about it—many of us start out each year making New Year's resolutions, yet very few of us finish and complete them, quitting somewhere along the way. Whatever you commit to doing, decide to finish and finish well. Gretchen Rubin said it like this: "What you do *every day* matters more than what you do *once in a while*."[2] First be consistent in your thinking, and that will lead to being consistent in your doing. Then if you say you are going to do something, do it. Have others hold you accountable. If you start something, finish it.

Finally, be humble. I don't know if anyone has ever broken this bad news to you, but leave me to be the one: you don't know everything. I had to learn this the hard way. We all have blind spots, things we do that we can't see but others can. To reach our potential and walk in discipline and greatness, we need people around us to call us out. Now, this is also important for you to hear: you shouldn't listen to everyone. Be careful who you listen to and who you allow to teach you and call you out. Those who enjoy criticizing you and putting you down don't deserve a seat at the table. There is a difference between criticism and feedback. Critics seek to tear you down. The right people to listen to are those who offer feedback to build you up. So with those you trust, give them permission to point out areas where you could grow. When they give you advice and point out areas you can work on, instead of being defensive or offended, be humble and grateful that they care enough to want you to be better. You don't need everyone on your team thinking you are the MVP all the time—that is not how you improve and become great.

If you are anything like me, discipline doesn't come naturally or easily. But by prioritizing your values over your feelings, you will learn to value what you want most over what you want in a moment. By prioritizing the important over the immediate, you will give your best to what deserves your best. By prioritizing right over easy, you will become brave, consistent, and humble. You are set apart for this moment in time, but you will need the discipline to walk it out. It's time to replace the constant pressing of the snooze button with the motivation and discipline to live a life you're proud of.

Challenges on Discipline

1. Write down three to five things you value and why. Before we can be disciplined and consistent, we must know what we value and why we value it. Once that list is established, write a vision and goal of where you want to go and who you want to be so that you know what you are working toward. Proverbs 29:18 (KJV) says, "Where there is no vision, the people perish."

2. Establish your priorities. Oh, I can't emphasize this one enough! Your day-to-day choices will reflect what you value most, and you will always prioritize what you find most valuable. When it comes to being disciplined, consistent, and excellent, we often have to sacrifice convenience and instant gratification for the sake of our long-term success. Once you have set your goal, make sure to write out your priorities, and don't let your feelings or the pressures of others mislead or manipulate them. You got this!

3. Create your own nonnegotiable schedule (NNS) and stick to it! In creating this plan, you will need to prioritize the most important first, then add in the time-sensitive tasks. Once you have created a schedule for yourself, give it to others so they can hold you accountable. My daily NNS looks like this:

    i. Spend at least fifteen minutes with God (spiritual).
    ii. Encourage someone (influential).
    iii. Do something active (physical).
    iv. Take at least ten minutes for myself to rest and meditate (emotional).
    v. Have a purposeful or challenging conversation with a friend or mentor (relational).

CHAPTER 5

DEAL WITH IT

Preparing for Your Future by Healing from Your Past

Standing in my high school hallway, I threw a bracelet at my boyfriend's head.

Yeah, it was just as dramatic as it sounds. Right after I threw the bracelet, the audience cheered, clapped, and went crazy! At least in my imagination.

I was in the ninth grade and had just grown out of the weird stage girls go through in middle school when they don't know what is happening to their bodies and are so confused about why things are changing and growing (or in my case not growing). Up until this point, I had never dated anyone. Until I met a guy I'll call Steve. Steve was insanely cute. He was a year older than I was and star quarterback of the football team. The only problem was that Steve was terribly shy and could barely string together a full sentence. It was like he was blind to his own beauty. Everyone else saw it, but he couldn't. Well, he showed some interest in me, and, man, did I feel special! Steve didn't usually flirt with anyone. I knew I had to date this guy. It would be just like in the movies. I would help him see all that he was and all that he could be! I imagined the whole *High School Musical* movie scenario in my mind, minus all the singing—we would be the *it* couple! This was all going on in my fifteen-year-old mind. Kind of pathetic, I know.

Steve and I started to date. He suddenly came out of his shell. I quickly discovered he was not only funny and had an outgoing personality but also loved to play basketball. Bonus! We dated for over six months, which at the time seemed like an eternity. In my mind, we were going to get married! But everything came crashing down one weekend.

That Monday morning at school felt like a scene from a dramatic movie. I was sitting in the cafeteria with my friends having lunch, giggling and having a great time, when my best friend walked in with a look on her face like something terrible had just happened. As she walked toward our lunch table, she kept her eyes locked on me. I knew immediately that she had bad news to tell me. Right in front of everyone, she blurted out, "Madison, I have to tell you—Steve not only cheated on you last night, but he made out with a random girl he doesn't even know." Are you kidding me? My face became red, and I felt like I would explode! I was so angry and so hurt. I thought, "I made him cool! And this is how he repays me? I let him into my heart and this is what he did to me?" Even though I was hurt and wanted to cry my eyes out, I hid my feelings and bottled them up because I didn't want him to know that his stupid decision had truly hurt me.

At first I acted like I didn't care: "Oh, his loss. What a bummer." Then I went to the bathroom to collect myself. I cried to my best friend, and we talked it out. I regained my composure and remembered how I deserved to be treated. Once I started thinking about that, I got worked up again. The bell rang for everyone to return to their classrooms. I walked out of the bathroom, and there was Steve, standing there with a pitiful puppy dog look on his face. We locked eyes. I rolled my eyes and let out a breath of irritation and anger. He came up to me pleading and begging for my forgiveness. Okay, maybe not begging, even though that's how I heard it in my head. He started giving me all the excuses in the world of why I should give him a second chance, how he messed up and didn't mean to hurt me. I stared at him with cold eyes. I let him go on and on until he finally finished. I responded, "Are you done?" He looked so confused. I said, "Good. And so are we." Then I took off the bracelet he had given me and chucked it at his head. Now, I know that wasn't the most mature way to handle the situation, but I was only fifteen. He wasn't harmed . . . well, maybe just his pride and his heart.

I broke up with him that day and began to move on with my life. What I didn't realize was that because I never thoroughly dealt with his unfaithfulness, I never fully healed. I put great effort into trying to forget this relationship and the hurt it had caused me, but I never forgave Steve, which is another way of saying I never gave the situation over to God. Instead, I swept my hurt under the rug, where, it turns out, it began festering. This unhealed hurt affected the rest of my relationships. I carried resentment toward him and all other boys into every relationship. I put up walls and refused to let anyone in. I would enter every relationship with a lack of trust, which resulted in my not being able to stay committed to a guy any longer than a few months. I would simply wait and expect something to go wrong. I was always on edge, ready for round two of the bracelet-throwing scenario.

Months after the breakup, one of my best friends looked at

me and said, "Are you going to let what Steve did to you affect the rest of your relationships? Pushing people away and putting up walls doesn't just keep you from getting hurt, it also keeps you from living, truly living." At first I felt defensive. I thought, "Steve didn't affect me. I don't care what he did. He has no hold over me. You don't know what you're talking about!" Then I realized she was right. I was a prisoner of my past.

After taking time to reflect on what she said, I was hit with this, and I hope it helps you: the only hurdle in your way is you, so jump over it. We've all had tough times and heartbreaks, but don't let your mind stay stuck. It's time to step into all that you can be! The chains of your past can't hold you. The people who rejected you can't limit you. Your circumstances can't stop you. Only you can.

> The only hurdle in your way is you, so jump over it.

I had to choose to break free, to walk forward, to see my reroutes as blessings instead of curses. I had to understand that those who walked out of my life were part of God's divine protection and redirection for something better. Life comes with a lot of highs and lows, and so many of those are out of our control. If we don't allow the lows to make us better, to grow and learn from them, then we went through all that pain for nothing. Life is too short to sit around feeling sorry for ourselves. We can instead find strength within to say to ourselves, "This hurts and this is painful—but I refuse to stay stuck here and let my past become my future."

You may be surprised to know that these feelings are common to many people, even many believers. Sometimes, out of a misunderstood sense of what repentance is, it feels right to pay for our past over and over again. We punish ourselves by calling to mind painful memories of our past mistakes, forgetting that God is a God of forgiveness and that we can trust him to set us free from our past. While being mindful of our shortcomings is good and healthy, fixating on them only convinces us that we are powerless to change. When we stay in this mindset, we either bury our pain and run from it, beat ourselves up about it, or blame others.

Whether you've been living in denial of the pain and pretending it doesn't exist or fixating and obsessing over your mistakes or the mistakes of another—both are ways of not "dealing with it." The first approach shoves what's painful into our subconscious, while the second approach keeps what's painful in our consciousness at all times. Neither of these approaches is a healthy way to deal with pain and struggle. When we don't deal with our pain, it continues to hurt us.

I don't know what you've been through or what's been done to you, and I won't try to pretend like I understand what you are feeling or what you are facing, but I will tell you that you will never experience the fullness of life and the potential of your future if you stay imprisoned to your past. Perry Noble said it like this in his book *Unleash!*: "If you don't let your past die, then it won't let you live."[1]

You are not your past. You are not what other people have said about you. You are not what other people believe you are. You are what you believe you are. Believe that you can get past this. Believe that you can keep going. Believe that you have something great to offer this world and that greatness lives inside you. Believe that you have what it takes to live a beautiful, meaningful life. Girl, it's time to *deal with it*.

It's vital to take steps in learning to deal with your past. I want to point out a few that helped me.

Awareness Is Key

If we want to be free, we have to be aware of and willing to confront the issues in our lives that have kept us bound. We don't want to walk around as prisoners, unaware that we are in chains.

Let's take some time to search our hearts right now and think about all the moments we have been deeply hurt: the most offensive, painful, and hurtful moments and the times we have reacted with anger, silent treatments, insecurity, or impatience. If we take a close look at those moments, we will notice there is a pattern: **often we respond in an immature manner not because of what is said but because of what is going on in our hearts.**

Anytime someone offends me or upsets me, I *try* (not always great at this) to take a second to ask myself *why* I feel hurt or offended. I always want to first make sure that there isn't something going on with me that caused me to react that way. If my response was appropriate, I believe it is healthy to then take a minute to sit down and talk to the person who hurt me.

The first step to dealing with your past is choosing not to bury it or run from it but to confront it and become aware of it. If not, it will affect your mood, your relationships, and your overall joy and contentment. Awareness may be uncomfortable at first, but in the end it will be your superpower.

Beautiful Scars

When I was little, I was pretty rough-and-tumble. Every week, I'd have new scars and bruises from monkey bar mishaps, participation in an intense game of tag, or overly competitive basketball games with my sisters. I was proud of my scars, my battle wounds that publicly showed I was a fighter and would do what it takes to win. But as I grew up, I started carrying around emotional scars from painful moments of rejection, heartbreak, and disappointment. I became less and less proud of my scars, covering them up as often as I could. The energy I spent trying to hide my scars kept me from truly healing. When we let our pain into the light of day and open up to others about our darkest moments, we realize that those moments, while part of us, don't define us. If we have the right perspective, scars are indicators of how far we've come.

I think being grateful for the scars is important; sometimes what caused them might have saved your life. Instead of being bitter and ashamed of them, embrace them—the scars are a part of your story. Forgiving people and seeking healing and freedom doesn't mean you forget everything that happened. You can notice that the scars are there without being ashamed that they are.

I want you to know that your scars are beautiful and not something to be ashamed of. What is in your past has already happened. You can't take it back or make it go away. Pretending it didn't happen will only cause more issues in the future. I promise you, there isn't anywhere deep enough for you to bury your pain. If you don't deal with your past, your past will deal with you. It happened. You have the scars to show for it. So where do you go from here?

Let your scars tell your story. Instead of trying to bury your past or run from it, use it to help other people. Use it to encourage those who may have lost even more than you did, and let them know they're not alone. We all have a story. We all have scars. Instead of hiding them away as something to be ashamed of, we can display them as evidence that we are fighters.

Maybe your past was glamorous. It was everything you wanted. To you, it was perfect. But then it was ripped away from you. Through a tragedy, rejection, or mistake you made, you lost everything. Your plans, your dreams all came crashing down. You sit here and think, "Right here, right now, this sucks. But back there, man, it was easy. It was fun. It was what I wanted." You feel like your best days are behind you. That's the best you'll ever get. There is no point in dreaming or putting yourself out there because you will only be disappointed. You feel stuck. Your past looks so dreamy because your present is so dreary. He was the one you wanted, he had your whole heart, but he walked away. You had your whole life planned, and it was going perfect, until an accident took away your greatest treasures. You were finally getting your life to a good place and then you lost your job. You had everything you wanted, but you screwed up on one bad night and lost everything you cared about.

I get it. I've been there. I still wrestle with those thoughts. I still have to speak this truth over myself even when I don't feel it: "My past was good, but greater days are still ahead of me. God is not finished with me yet!" It's true. I know life can be hard and depressing when you feel like you have nothing to look forward to and every day is the same and you feel so alone in it all. I have been here. But I want to remind you that your present season is not your forever season. Just because this is your situation right now doesn't mean this is how it will always be. Every season of life is different. Sometimes you're in the wilderness, sometimes the mountaintops, sometimes the valley, sometimes the desert. But whatever season you find yourself in, it is not permanent. There is something to be taken from this season and something to be learned. Don't miss it. You will need it for where God is taking you next. You have to tell yourself, even when you don't feel it, even when you don't see it, to keep pressing in, keep trusting and believing. You may not see anything changing. You may not see what you want to see right now. But refuse to believe the lie that your better days are behind you. In the book of Philippians, we are encouraged and reminded that God will always finish what he starts: "He who began a good work in you will carry it on to completion until the day of Christ Jesus" (Philippians 1:6).

Your present season is not your forever season.

I want to encourage you wherever you are—shameful or embarrassed of your past, or envious of your past. Don't stay stuck there. Your past is your past for a reason. It is meant to be learned from and remembered but is not meant to be lived in.

Next Play

When I first started playing basketball on the varsity team, I was in seventh grade. I looked up to a girl on our team named Olivia. She wasn't the most skilled player on the team, but she certainly outworked and outhustled every person on the court. Her grit factor was a ten out of ten. She would dive into the bleachers just to get a loose ball. Sometimes she would fall to the ground so hard I thought she would have to be rushed to the hospital, but seconds later she would pop right back up again. If the coach (my dad) insisted she needed to come out for a second, she would always look at him and shake her head. "No, coach, I'm good!" Many bruises later, my dad finally made her wear knee pads for every game because Olivia's legs were black and blue from the number of loose balls she would run after.

Olivia often made mistakes on the court, but rather than becoming discouraged or giving up, she wrote "next play" on her basketball shoe and would read it out loud before every game. One day I asked her why she wrote that on her shoe. She told me, "I may make a stupid mistake on a play, but I don't want that one play to cost me the rest of the game. So I write it to remind myself not to stay stuck in what I lost back there but to pick my head up and move on to the next play." I thought that was profound, not only in sports but also in life.

In sports and in life, I am hard on myself. I'm easily angered or frustrated or caught up in what happened back there. Whether a situation was my fault or someone else's, sometimes moving on can be hard. Olivia reminded me that no matter what mistake I made, it didn't have to determine the outcome of the rest of the game. I can choose to move on and focus on the next play. So I decided to write "next play" on my shoe so that every game, I would look down and remember not to dwell on my past mistakes but to focus on how I could be better for the next play. Everyone on our team picked up on this principle, and because of that attitude, we went on to win a championship.

You might not need to write "next play" on your shoe, but do try to keep that mindset. The mistake you made or the thing that happened to you in the past doesn't have to define you or hold you back any longer. You can choose to move forward, and you can choose to have the "next play" mentality. We will all experience tough breaks, bad days, and disappointments. We will all make mistakes and fall short. We will all fail at some point. Even the most successful people have experienced these setbacks, if not even more often and to a higher degree. When you pursue purpose, excellence, and greatness, you will also experience nos, setbacks, missed shots, losses, and tough opponents. When you're dealing with people, you're going to experience hurt, betrayal, disappointment, and unmet expectations. But you don't have to stay stuck there. Let it make you stronger. Learn from it. Keep going.

Sometimes people believe that by putting up walls, they keep out all the bad, which might be true. But they also keep out the good. Building walls, we keep ourselves free not only from pain and rejection but also from love and life-giving relationships.

We often get so frustrated and down on ourselves when we make a mistake—especially when we trip over the one hurdle that we thought we were finally past. You decided you wouldn't go back to that person, but you had a weak moment and went back to him. You decided you weren't going to look at that website, but temptation got the best of you. You decided you weren't going to hang around that group of friends anymore, but you got lonely so you went back to what you were used to. Whatever it is, we like to punish ourselves for our mistakes. We feel that is what we deserve. "I shouldn't have done that. I am better than that! I thought I was past that! I don't deserve God's blessings. I don't deserve God's forgiveness." We go through life with this mindset, but really it is selfish and dishonors God. It is what I call the helplessness mindset. What we may have lost in a moment of weakness should not keep us bound with a defeated mindset.

Don't let your past mistakes control you. Take control over your mistakes. You do that by going through the healing process: owning that mistake, repenting, dealing with it, and then using it to help other people. Hiding your mistakes and keeping them to yourself helps no one, including you. Punishing yourself the rest of your life does not help. No matter what you did, no matter what has been done to you, nothing is too big, too dark, too scary, or too impossible for God. Don't stay stuck in the past. Whether it was full of good or full of bad, let it shape you, inspire you, train you, and prepare you for what's to come.

> Don't let your past mistakes control you. Take control over your mistakes.

Your past and your scars can be used for good. They can help others and bring them hope and encouragement. Romans 8:28 reminds us, "In all things God works for the good of those who love him, who have been called according to his purpose."

You can't step into your full potential without confronting and breaking free from your past. Because you are a made-for-this-moment woman, embrace how you are made, allow your past to shape and grow you but not define you, and choose daily to walk in freedom. If you want a bright future, make sure you are doing the work of dealing with your past now so that it won't hold you back or trip you up when your moment comes.

Challenges on Dealing with Your Past

1. Be honest with yourself about the chains and pains of your past. Awareness is always the first step to change. To fix, move past, or deal with something, you have to be aware of the issue and the root of it.

2. Remember, nobody's perfect. When I say this, I automatically think about the Hannah Montana song. (If you are like me, you are now currently singing this song in your head.) Everyone comes with baggage and a flawed past. You are not alone.

3. Remind yourself of the truth, and speak words of life over your past mistakes and your current struggles. You are not defined by your past. You are not what you have done. You are not what has been done to you. You are more than enough. Write it on your mirror or have it tattooed, I don't care—just don't ever forget it. This truth is what you need to cling to when your past haunts you.

CHAPTER 6

THE PRICE OF
UNFORGIVENESS

How to Respond to Offense

For ten weeks I wasn't able to talk with any of my friends or family, so after returning from filming *The Bachelor*, I couldn't wait to spend time with my friends back home. One of my close friends invited me over for lunch, and I was beyond excited to visit with her and catch up on all that I had missed over the last few months. During the conversation, she shared some information with me that I wasn't expecting. She told me that one of my close friends had spread rumors about me while I was gone. I sat there in shock as I listened to her repeat all the hurtful words that my "friend" had told to many people. I tried to play it cool and act as if it didn't bother me. But it did.

I left that lunch feeling defeated. How could my friend say these things about me? How could she betray me like this? The words played over and over in my mind. I started wondering if all my other friends felt the same way. That's when the walls went up, walls to protect me from her and anyone else that shared in the gossip.

Unaware that I had received this information, this same friend reached out to me by text and asked if we could meet for lunch. The nerve. I refused to respond. Not only would I not have lunch with her, but I would not text her back. Better yet, I would never speak to her again. She offended me and I was unyielding. She hurt me once; I would not let her do it again.

Then one day during my morning devotions, I read a phrase out of a book called *Living in Freedom Every Day* that caused me to rethink the situation: "In light of all that I have been forgiven, can I release the person who has wronged me? Would I trade my forgiveness from God for the right to hold a person accountable for their offense towards me?"[1] Wow! I knew in that moment that I needed to reach back out to this friend, not because she deserved my forgiveness but because I needed to, for my own personal healing and freedom.

I sent my friend a text and told her I would like to meet for lunch. And as much as I would have liked to get riled up and spew out how offended I was, I set those impulses aside. I shared that she hurt me to the core, and she admitted with regret that she did say those things and asked me to forgive her. And I chose to. Right then and there. Having an honest conversation allowed us to put it all out on the table, then *clear* the table, so we could move on. We spent the rest of the time talking about our families and everything that had happened since we last saw each other. Whether she deserved to get off the hook that easily wasn't the issue. My ability to get over the offense and move past it was what I needed to resolve.

I will admit that forgiving her wasn't easy. And it did not happen overnight. I knew I couldn't do it if I relied on my feelings. It was a choice, a daily choice, that I would have to make. I realized that I can't always control what someone says about me, but I can control how I respond.

Sometimes forgiving someone may feel like a sign of weakness. You don't want to seem weak, so you continue to harbor anger, resentment, and bitterness toward them. But forgiving someone, even if they don't deserve or ask for it, is the greatest demonstration of strength!

Whom do you need to forgive? Most of us have fallen victim to words and deeds of others that caused indescribable pain and resentment. Abuse, neglect, betrayal, abandonment, and offensive words directed at us often lead to bitterness and unforgiveness that remain in our hearts long after the wrongdoing takes place. When someone hurts you through words or actions, unforgiveness may feel fair. After all, they should have to pay for the offense, right? But by holding on to unforgiveness, you end up being the one held captive, not the person who offended you.

We all deal with offenses against us. The question is how are we going to handle them? If we don't learn to deal with offense and instead cling to unforgiveness, we will end up in our own self-constructed prisons. The way we deal with offenses will have a direct impact on the direction of our future. Choosing forgiveness and moving forward is less about God "rewarding" us for practicing forgiveness and more about getting out of our own way so we don't let bitterness hold us back from the good plans God has for us.

> By holding on to unforgiveness, you end up being the one held captive.

Forgiving but Not Minimizing the Offense

Have you ever been told, "Forgive and forget"? This insinuates that you are supposed to sweep transgressions under the rug and act like they never happened. Sometimes I wish it were that simple, but it never is. When we bury our pain, mistakes, and hurts and "forget" about them, they end up haunting us later. Just because you aren't thinking about or talking about an offense doesn't mean it isn't there. Just because you swept it under the rug doesn't mean it disappeared. It didn't. And it won't.

Lysa TerKeurst, one of my favorite authors, has written a whole book about these ideas, called *Forgiving What You Can't Forget*. She powerfully puts the importance of forgiveness in perspective: "Living in the comfort of peace is so much better than living in the constraints of unforgiveness."[2] By trying to forget, you often think you are doing yourself a favor, but you're actually doing yourself a disservice. That thing that you chose to bury or forget about will always be there until you choose to be courageous enough to confront it, face it head on, and go through the healing process. Until then, you will find yourself struggling in relationships and not knowing why, having trust issues, and reacting instead of responding. Many think that by doing this, they keep themselves from getting hurt again. They think, "I just won't care about anything. I'll forget about it. I'll leave before I get left." Not only is this a sad way to live but it also keeps you attached and imprisoned to the very thing that you told yourself to "forget about." This is not what it looks like to live in "the comfort of peace," as Lysa says.

For so long, I didn't know how to walk in freedom or let my heart heal or what that process would even entail. I didn't know how to let go of my past pains and hurts so that when I thought about those moments or those people, anger and hurt didn't arise again. I wanted to be at a place where I could share about my past without it triggering me again. I wanted my story and my struggles to help and encourage others. But I didn't know how to get there. Maybe that is you.

Let's be clear: there is a difference between instantly forgiving and walking in forgiveness. Forgiving someone happens all at once. But you may wake up the next morning dealing with just as much anger or hurt or shame or guilt. That pain doesn't go away with the magical words, "I forgive you." **While forgiveness is a decision that happens in a moment, choosing to walk out that forgiveness is a process that happens little by little.** Lysa TerKeurst says it like this: "Forgiveness is both a decision and a process. You make the decision to forgive the facts of what happened. But then you must also walk through the process of forgiveness for the impact those facts had on you."[3] Some days you will feel really good—you have moved on and you're in a great place. Then, *bam*, out of nowhere your feelings and thoughts run wild. Anger rises. Pain brings you back to your knees.

Good days and bad days will come. I wish I could tell you the pain goes away completely. But it doesn't. Something will be said or done that triggers something of the past. You see someone you haven't seen in a while. You hear a song that reminds you of that person. You scroll on Instagram and see a photo that brings back memories. You pass by a house you have dodged for a while. Or maybe you lie in bed at night and your thoughts run wild with the pains of yesterday. When something triggers pain from your past, please know that even this is part of the healing process. You're not "doing forgiveness wrong."

I think we have the hardest time forgiving when the people who let us down are the ones we're closest to or the ones we've given our hearts to. That's when the offense stings. That's when it's hurtful. Trust me, I get it. I feel you. I have had many people I thought I could trust and count on to be there for me, but instead they easily walked away and talked about me all the way out the door. That was hard on me for a long time. I thought maybe there was something else I could have done. Maybe it was my fault they walked away. Did I do something wrong? I had to learn that sometimes people will walk out of your life. Sometimes people will leave for no reason. Let them go. If they can leave that easily, then you don't need them. Those kinds of people are in your life for a season but are not meant to be in it forever. If you needed them to get to where you're going, they would still be around.

Choosing to forgive is not always easy, especially when we have been hurt and wounded and left alone. We tend to be able to see only what is right in front of us, but God can see the whole picture. You may not understand the reason for the heartbreak, but one day you will thank God for it all. What I used to see as a disappointment I now see as the hand of God. The choice to heal is one you'll never regret.

> The choice to heal is one you'll never regret.

Moving Past Offense

My close friend and I were having a conversation one night when out of the blue she said, "Madi, don't ever take the relationship you have with your dad for granted." Then she opened up and told me some very personal things about her childhood. What she shared with me was an amazing illustration of the power of forgiveness. The following story is her testimony.

My dad wasn't there the day I was born. He wasn't there when I started kindergarten. He wasn't there to teach me how to ride a bike. He wasn't there to hug me when I had a bad day or to cheer for me when I played sports. He wasn't there for my high school graduation, and he was not there to walk me down the aisle on my wedding day. I remember watching other girls with their dads growing up, wishing just once I had a dad to run to after school, to dance with at the daddy-daughter dance, to teach me to throw the ball in the yard, or to tell me I was beautiful in my prom dress.

I never told anyone how desperately I longed for a father. I just kept it buried deep inside. Over time I grew to resent my father for not being there in the moments I needed him. But what angered me most was the way he treated my mother. He battled with alcoholism and had multiple affairs. He would show up at our house, often drunk, begging for my mother to take him back. She wanted to believe that he was sincere and had changed, so she would give him another chance to prove himself. And every time he would end up physically and mentally abusing her, right in front of us kids. Then he would vanish again, leaving my mother more broken than she was before.

My mother worked several jobs to be able to provide for four children. She did everything she could to make sure we had food and a roof over our heads. But with no help from my father, it wasn't always enough. There were times we did not have any food in the house or money to go buy any, so we would go outside and gather pecans or berries just to have something to eat. Sometimes my mother couldn't afford to pay the electric bill, so we would have to load up in the car and drive to my grandmother's until payday. I cannot imagine the shot to my mother's pride. The hardest memory I have was when I made cheerleader for the first time, and I saw the look on my mother's face when she had to tell me that I would not be able to cheer at the first game because she did not have the money to buy the required cheer shoes. I saw the devastation and pain in her eyes. We both cried. And it made me despise my father even more.

For over thirty years, I held unforgiveness and bitterness toward my father. Until the day I joined a Bible study and the leader spoke on the power of forgiveness. She mentioned that only by letting go and forgiving would I ever experience true freedom. That I should not wait for him to apologize, because by doing that, I hold myself hostage to the very one who hurt me, and I place my freedom in his hands. The leader explained that forgiving the person who hurt me did not mean that I must reconcile with that person. She said, "It takes two to reconcile but only one to forgive."

To be honest, I did not want to forgive him. I wanted him to suffer miserably and feel pain like I had. Like my mother had. I wanted him to hurt like he hurt us. But one thing the leader said kept coming back to my memory—because I had been forgiven, I had to forgive. Even if my dad didn't deserve it. As long as I harbored unforgiveness, I was the one bound, not him. And if I continued to choose not to deal with it, it had the power to paralyze my ability to live, love, and be loved.

I decided this was something I must do if I was ever going to live a healthy, fulfilled life. I knew if I waited until I felt like forgiving, I would never do it. So I picked up the phone and called him. Full of emotions and completely vulnerable, I simply said, "Dad, I just wanted to tell you that I forgive you and I love you, and from this day forward I will no longer hold unforgiveness in my heart toward you."

I immediately felt free from the enormous weight I had carried for so many years. I knew this was a life-changing moment for me. But even though I felt immediate relief, forgiving my dad is something I will have to do for the rest of my life. When feelings of hate try to crowd my mind or something triggers a memory, I simply say a prayer of blessing for him, knowing that even though forgiveness may not change him, it changes me.

It must have been hard for my friend to open up and share this story with me. But I've learned that there is power in being transparent and letting people into the most vulnerable places of your heart. I encouraged her to share her story with more people. So she decided to lead her own Bible study. During one of the meetings, she told the girls in her group the same story she shared with me. After she finished, one of the girls was weeping uncontrollably. She asked her if she would like to share what was bothering her. The girl went on to tell how for over twenty years she carried the weight of a secret that kept her in bondage. My friend said the group could feel the pain as she told about how someone she loved and trusted sexually abused her as a child. She told how the unforgiveness that she held on to had affected her other relationships for years. That night, in that moment, she chose to make the life-changing decision to forgive her abuser. Since that night, she has counseled countless girls who have been through similar abuse situations and has helped them in their journey to forgiveness and freedom.

Here are some practical steps for moving past offense:

1. **Decide to forgive.** Action to forgive has to first be initiated on your end, regardless of whether they deserve it or will appreciate it. But walking in forgiveness will require more than simply saying, "I forgive this person." It will mean choosing to forgive daily, even when painful feelings of the offense resurface. At times this may be extremely difficult and even seem impossible, but if you decide to forgive and follow through, it will be worth it down the road.

2. **Pray for your offender.** This may seem strange and will certainly be tough to do, but it will lead to joy and freedom in your own heart and can even open the eyes and heart of the offender.

3. **Give it to God.** You may feel that you can never fully forgive someone who has deeply wounded you, but if you ask God to help you, he will give you the strength and grace you need to let go. This is when you have to trust. You have done your part in forgiving and praying, now leave the rest up to God. Healing may take some time; be okay with the process.

Friend, if you don't learn to deal with unforgiveness and the walls you've put up, you will find yourself in a prison. It's not the offender that is held captive, it's you. As hard as it is to let go of an offense and give it to God, holding on to what someone has done to you will always come at a greater cost. It's not worth it. You hold the power to say, "Enough." **Choose to forgive, and watch how the past releases its hold on your future.**

Challenges on Forgiveness

1. Decide today that no matter what others say or do, you will respond with love, truth, and grace because you know who you are and no one and nothing is ever worth compromising that. You can't always control what someone says to you or about you, but you can decide how to respond.

2. Embrace the healing process. True healing takes time. We live in a world that wants everything immediately. We often think that if something takes time, it must not be working, or it must not be worth it. It is actually the opposite. Often the longer we have to wait, the greater the reward. Don't give up. Healing is also a choice, not a feeling. You have to choose daily to forgive and walk in healing.

3. Let go of the pain. Many of us carry around hurt, pain, and bitterness as if unforgiveness is revenge or payback for the person who hurt us, yet we are only hurting ourselves. Don't let unforgiveness rob you of the blessing of today. Only by letting go of that pain and choosing to forgive can we be truly free.

CHAPTER 7

WHO DO YOU WANT TO BE?

Anchoring Yourself in Your
Identity *Before* the Pressure Hits

I became besties with a stranger in Forever 21.

When I was younger, one of my favorite places to shop was Forever 21. I would always end up in the dressing room with a ton of cute outfits. On this particular day, I was in a hurry and had one goal: find the perfect denim jacket. I knew exactly what I wanted: distressed denim with a few rips in the back. I wasn't having much luck finding a jacket but discovered several cute dresses that I decided to try on. You know how it is: you can never find what you're looking for but always find what you don't need. When I walked into my dressing room, I dropped all the dresses I was holding and squealed with excitement! Hanging on the hook was the coolest denim jacket I had ever seen. Distressed. Ripped. It even had black leather on the collar that gave it more character. Destiny. It was meant for me. I could have picked any dressing room, but I had chosen this one. And the jacket I needed was right there waiting. Now all I needed to do was make sure it fit, and it would be mine.

I tried it on. It fit like a glove. Could this be more perfect? I took several pictures and sent them to my mom to get her approval. Of course, she fell in love with it just as I had.

I forgot all about the dresses and decided I would make only one purchase that day. I couldn't wait to show off my jacket to all my friends. I had already imagined wearing it to at least three outings.

I decided to keep the jacket on and wear it out to sport it and show it off. When I walked out of the dressing room, I noticed a girl staring at me all weird. At first I thought, "Oh, she's jealous of my jacket—I would be too!" But she kept looking, so I became a little nervous. I asked her if everything was okay, and she said, "Well, you walked into my dressing room, and now you're wearing my jacket." I don't think I spoke for a solid three minutes. How could this be true? This jacket was destined for me! Sad and embarrassed, I took off the jacket and slowly handed it to her. I guess it was the pitiful look on my face that made her feel sorry for me. She took the jacket and then sympathetically said, "Girl, why don't you follow me?" She led me out of the store and down the mall to Macy's. Then she took me to the rack that had more jackets just like hers. We laughed and joked about the situation and even took pictures of the two of us in our matching jackets.

Now, I don't recommend going into other people's dressing rooms and trying on strangers' jackets (even though I made a friend that way). I do, however, love telling the story, and I still have the pictures of me and the jacket of my dreams. It's a funny story, but it reminds me of a human tendency that runs far deeper. How often do we try on other people's lives, just as I tried on this girl's jacket, because they look better than our own? We like what they have—the fun parties, the cool friends, the perfect family—so we want those things for ourselves. We may also become jealous of their skills, whether it be sports, fashion, photography, and so on, and we try to operate in their gift set because it is "cooler." When we do this, we are constantly looking at others and never within ourselves. We see only what they have to offer and not what makes us unique and valuable.

A huge part of being ready for the moments ahead is establishing a sense of self that can't be shaken. There are a lot of obstacles to overcome as we struggle to be truly confident. Pressures, questions of purpose, and misplaced sources of identity can get in our way. Just as I stumbled into someone else's dressing room, we get stuck staring in the mirror, wearing clothes that don't belong to us. But it's time to clear the road and make our way to a new understanding of our identity. It's time to see the beauty within ourselves. It's time to "wear our own jacket" proudly! It's time to know who we are and what we have to offer. It's time to discover how valuable we truly are, because only then can we walk in the fullness of all God has to offer!

Who Is the World Telling Me to Be?

"Stay true to who you are, Madi." Those were the last words my dad said before I boarded the plane to leave for *The Bachelor*. Those words carried more power than my dad may have realized. Going into filming, I had no way of knowing if I would be accepted for who I was by Peter or the other girls on the show. I knew there would be moments when I would be tested in my ability to stay true to myself.

For many years I allowed the labels people placed on me to have influence over my life and the decisions I made. Knowing this was something I had struggled with in the past, I held on to those words my dad challenged me with, as I knew I might be stepping into an environment that would challenge me to the core.

Thankfully, as I reflect now, the girls and Peter were accepting of who I was and encouraged me to stay true to myself, yet that wasn't always the case when I was growing up.

What labels have you allowed others to place on you? Or what labels have you placed on yourself?

Most of my life I have battled the pressure to conform. I have often wondered, "Why did God make me this way?" I am strong-willed, competitive, and fiery! But a lot of the people I was around didn't have that same stubborn fight in them. Because of my strong-willed nature and fighter spirit, I was the hardest for my parents to raise, requiring much more discipline and attention than my sisters. Growing up, I received many frowny faces in my preschool classes because I was always too loud and led my classmates to games rather than work. In middle school and high school, I felt different from most of the girls in my friend group; they saw me as the confrontational one. I fought against feeling like something was wrong with me. I would put labels on myself: strong-willed, "too much," stubborn, fiery, and misfit. I worked hard to constantly get approval and acceptance from people. Because I wasn't sure who I was, I hoped others would tell me by labeling me something better than I labeled myself.

The opinions of others and a wrong view of self can have this effect on us, pressing in on us from all sides until we have no room to be ourselves. Whether you feel lonely or left out, rejected or rebellious, impatient to grow up or scared of the future, misunderstood or desperate to fit in, I see you. I've been there.

Everywhere we look, there is so much pressure that we may feel broken, lost, and desperate to find our identity and validation in anything or anyone who will accept us.

We turn to a boy, but he leaves us even more rejected and empty than before. We then turn to "friends," but they leave us feeling even more alone. We tell ourselves, "After this drink, I will feel much better," only to find ourselves broken and depressed. There is no one to turn to, so we look to social media, but it leaves us feeling like no matter what we do or what we give, it will never be enough. Everywhere we turn—food, alcohol, boyfriends, you name it—we can't seem to find the answer to these questions: Who am I? Why am I here? Does anyone care?

Arden Bevere, a dear friend of mine, wrote a book called *Redefined*, and throughout that book he confronts the negative labels we allow ourselves to carry, and he encourages us to redefine the labels with God's Word. Arden says, "Our generation is called to change the world. I truly believe that. But to step into our full potential and true identity, we must *redefine* the way we see ourselves. We must listen to the right voices and believe the right words. We must confront and reject the labels that limit us and restore the calling of God that defines us."[1]

I share all this because I see the warning signs flashing in my own life and in the lives of many other girls I know. This pressure to conform threatens who we are at our very core, and if we aren't quick to catch ourselves, we can easily be shaped into people we didn't plan on becoming. What I don't want is to see a generation of girls who have been pressured to perform or follow the next trend for so long that they don't even have a voice for themselves.

Have you ever been overwhelmed with the pressures of the world and the pressure to be someone else? So much so that you've lost your sense of identity—you feel you're the same as the next girl? I've had many days of feeling like I'm grasping at straws for some deeper sense of myself or my purpose. My guess is you've felt this too.

Have you ever lost something that you spend hours looking for but can't seem to find it anywhere, and it drives you crazy? I can't tell you how many times I have lost or misplaced my keys, phone, wallet, or purse. It happens more than I would like to admit. Shoot, I have even lost my car in parking lots! How can you lose a car? Or there's my least favorite scenario: have you ever had your luggage lost at the airport, and you have to sit and wait for hours or even days, hoping they can track down your bag and return it to you? It's the worst!

One time on *The Bachelor*, our luggage got lost. We had just arrived at the airport in Costa Rica super late at night only to find out that none of our bags had made it. It was beyond frustrating; we were tired and exhausted. You know those people who are smart packers? The prepared travelers? The people who pack their toiletries, undergarments, and an extra pair of clothes in their carry-on just in case? Yeah, that's not me. The airline told us it could take a couple of days for the bags to make it out to us since the resort we were staying at was in the middle of nowhere, over two hours from the airport. We all climbed aboard our bus with nothing in our hands and rode off to our resort. Having no toothbrushes, makeup, hairbrushes, or clean clothes—all while being filmed on national television for millions to see—we had quite an interesting time. So for two days we kicked it in our travel clothes until our bags finally arrived.

If you've ever traveled and had to deal with recovering a piece of lost luggage, you know how frustrating the process can be. But if losing your clothes for your trip is a pain, imagine how frustrating—or even scary—losing your identity can be. Maybe you've misplaced who you are for long enough that you're wandering around, just waiting for some suitcase full of yourself to show up in the jungle. But here's a secret: you don't have to depend on someone else to deliver your worth to your door. Your identity— who you are at your very core—comes from God. **And when you know that your identity is not dependent on who everyone else is telling you to be, it can't ever be lost or stolen from you.**

Not everyone will value your gifts, passions, heart, and dreams. They won't see your worth. But if *you* value you, if you know who you are, what others do or don't do, say or don't say, doesn't matter. Knowing who we are deep down is easier said than done. So how can we find hope when we are constantly being pushed an identity-altering narrative for our lives?

Who Does God Say I Am?

What is identity? How can we discover it and know our worth and value?

Identity is defined as the qualities and beliefs that distinguish a person. Our identity is the core of who we are. Everything we do and say stems from our confidence in who we believe we are. We make decisions or take certain courses of action because of where we place our identity. Bottom line, our identity affects every area of our lives. This is why pinpointing the source of our identity is so important.

All throughout the Bible we are reminded that we were made in the image of God. As women, we are described as daughters of the Most High God. Everything that we are, every perfect and imperfect quality we possess, was created with intention, thought, and purpose by the God of the universe.

The truth is, no one and nothing can take away our God-given identity, but it is up to us to accept our inherent worth and identity.

When you don't know your worth, you are like a paper in the wind—you go wherever the wind blows, you allow the circumstances around you to dictate where you go and who you are rather than searching deep within yourself and discovering who you are and why you were put on this earth.

It is up to us to accept our inherent worth and identity.

Many pressures and forces try to define who we are. When we bend to those pressures, our view of ourselves gets hazy, and we have a harder time seeing the image of God looking back at us in the mirror. **Friends, don't let others' inability to see your worth make you question how you see it.** So while many are losing their sense of self, how can we be the exception?

You might not like my answer. You don't have to believe what I'm going to say. But all I can share is what I believe. There is only One who can satisfy you, fill you, sustain you, and tell you who you are: The One who created you. The One who died for you. The One who made you worthy and calls you worthy. And the One who hasn't stopped pursuing you and loving you since the moment you took your first breath—actually, even before that!

You don't have to prove yourself to anyone. Not to that guy, your boss, strangers, the world. You don't have to perform to be loved. Love isn't performance based, and if it is for you, it isn't true love. You don't have to prove your worth. You are worthy whether you ever see it within yourself or accept it for yourself because God himself calls you worthy. The moment you stop performing is the moment you start truly living. Here you find peace, contentment, and joy. Here you discover who you truly are and why you were created the way you were.

That doesn't mean you'll never face another moment of pressure in your life—there's still plenty more to be said about my own moments of pressure both in private and in front of millions. But rooting our sense of self in God's love for us is crucial. Our identity must be anchored in him above all else. But you're probably thinking, "Madi, it's one thing to say I don't have to perform to be loved, but it's quite another thing to believe it." Hear me out: no one can tell you more about who you are than the One who created you. **Our identity has less to do with who the world says we are and more to do with who God is and who he says we are.**

> The moment you stop performing is the moment you start truly living.

Once we know where our identity can be found, the fruits of our lives will reflect what we believe. You have to decide for yourself where you find your identity. But I believe you will never be content until you place it in the One who created you. Only in believing what he says about you can you become truly confident and content in who you are. There is no need to try harder and fake it until you make it. Rather, take a deep breath, take off the mask, and surrender to him and let him show you who you are. If you're always asking, "Who am I?" I hope by the end of this chapter that you will be able to turn this question into a statement: This is who I am.

Who Do I Want to Be?

One day in my college dorm room, I knew I was ready to offer my whole self to God. I didn't want the opinions of others or the social pressures to conform to define me. I had tried all that before, and it didn't work. I wanted my identity to come from God. So on a Thursday afternoon, I hit my knees and prayed, "God, tell me who I am. I'm tired of trying to live up to this standard or be someone I'm not. I'm tired of feeling that I am a mistake or that something went terribly wrong with me. I want to embrace how you made me and be confident in the gifts and passions inside me. I'm tired of comparing myself to the other women around me, wondering why their lives seem so much easier. You don't make mistakes, and there is a reason I am the way I am. Help me see myself the way that you see me."

This prayer changed everything for me. I began reading God's Word and writing his truth of who I am all over my mirror and journals. Once I realized who God says I am, I had a choice to make. Do I want to accept and believe this as the ultimate truth of who I am? The answer: Yes! I stopped viewing myself through the labels of the world, the boxes other people placed me in, and my own insecurities. I stopped believing the lies that I was unwanted, too different, complicated, and not good enough. I started embracing and loving the way God wired me. I didn't feel sorry for myself anymore. I stopped comparing my gifts and strengths with those of others. I stopped resenting how different I felt. I embraced all that I was and all that God told me I am. I still pray through those areas of weakness because they never completely go away. But when I finally came to a place of true contentment in how God made me, my relationships got better, my daily attitude and perspective improved, and I was able to grow in confidence in who I was—how God made me—and in my purpose.

If you've wondered, "Who am I?" or, "Who do I want to be?" I hope I can offer some practical insight into how I've come to answer those questions with confidence. First, let me say that this assurance didn't happen instantly; there were many "behind the scenes" moments of asking questions, wiping away tears, dealing with frustration, studying God's Word, and praying Scripture over myself until I finally believed what God said about me. As you've read, for years I struggled with my sense of self. But since that prayer I prayed in my dorm, I've been able to implement a few habits that you might be able to put into practice. With that in mind, here are a few questions to think through.

Ask yourself:

Who does the world say I am?
Where do I find my sense of self right now?

I'd encourage you to get out a journal and spend some time exploring your answers to these questions. You might feel like you're too loud and ambitious or too quiet and timid. You might find your sense of self in your starting position on your team or in your GPA or in your boyfriend or in the number of likes you got on your latest social media post. However you answer, whether you feel confident in who you are or totally lost, it's important to establish a baseline understanding of how you view yourself and how you think others view you.

Then ask yourself:

Who do I want to be?
What do I need to change in my life to push back against the
    harmful pressures I face?

Once you've identified where you're placing your identity, you then have to look ahead to where you want to be. I want to be anchored in my purpose and strong and confident in the Madi that God made me to be. To get there, I needed to evaluate how I engaged on social media, who I listened to, and whether I was intentional about filling my heart with the truth of God's Word. Take some time again to write out the answers to these questions. Who do you want to be, and what's getting in the way of that?

We're going to talk more specifically about how to grow in confidence and defeat the monster of comparison in later chapters, but for now, start setting your sights on the person you want to be.

Lastly, keep asking yourself:

Who does God say I am?
How can I apply his truth to my life?

This isn't a one-time question. It's one we should return to over and over. When we ask the questions of identity, we are preparing the soil of our hearts so that God can plant and cultivate his truth. Returning to the question of who God says we are is like tending and watering a garden. Knowing the truth of our worth will bear fruit for years to come. I often go back and reflect on that moment of praying in my dorm room because it was a benchmark moment for me. It was a time when I paused to recognize I had lost part of myself, but I knew it was time to ask God to help me find the Madison he created me to be. Maybe that kind of prayer scares you, but I know that when we pause to listen to God, he will answer. In that moment, these truths became clear to me:

- We are made in the likeness and image of God.
  (Genesis 1:27)
- We are his prized possessions. (James 1:18 NLT)
- We are his ambassadors. (2 Corinthians 5:20)
- We are citizens of the kingdom of heaven. (Philippians 3:20)
- We are united with God and one with him in spirit.
  (1 Corinthians 6:17)

These are truths I keep going back to. On hard days, on good days, on normal boring days, I am loved by God, made in his image, and have a purpose, which is to love him and love others. It's a simple truth, but it takes work to know it deeply and live out of that belief. As you reflect on these questions, I hope you will find encouragement in these words and begin the work of being rooted in Christ. **Because when you become who God says you are, you won't be easily shaken. You'll be ready for the challenges—the moments—that come your way.**

Finding Light

So far we've talked about who others say we are and becoming who God says we are. But something we haven't talked about is the times in life that can rock you to your core and uproot you. Sometimes difficult circumstances and trauma try to latch on to our identity, and we can start to think that those things define who we are. Instead of letting our circumstances shape and grow us, we let them have the final word. The beautiful thing about letting Christ define our identity is that all the junk we go through can't shake his love for us—ever.

There is one person in my life who has shown me this truth repeatedly. I have a friend, Hannah, who at six years of age was diagnosed with an autoimmune condition called Crohn's. It progressed and got so bad that she had to be hospitalized. This disease is only a small part of her struggles. When she was only two years old, her parents divorced, and her dad stayed in England, while Hannah and her mom moved back to the States. They struggled financially, and with barely enough money to survive, they lived off food stamps until she was about seven. Then Hannah's mom remarried. Hannah's stepdad turned out to be verbally and emotionally abusive to both Hannah and her mom, which caused

Hannah to slip into depression and anxiety. Hannah's mom didn't know how to stand up for herself. One day Hannah found her mom unconscious on the floor from trying to take her own life. That day will forever be engrained in Hannah's memory.

Hannah and her mom also lived in a rough part of town, known for its drug deals, gangs, and violence. She was so ashamed of her life that she lied to her friends about where she lived. When they would come to pick her up, she'd run to a nearby neighborhood and stand in front of a house that wasn't hers. She ended up developing obsessive-compulsive disorder in the sixth grade as a coping mechanism for the trauma she was facing. All these labels fought to define who she was: unwanted, unloved, sick, poor, depressed, and anxious.

Hannah's identity was under fire from the time she was a little girl. Her circumstances and people around her deemed her unfit, unworthy, and unwanted. She believed these lies about herself most of her life. After high school, the crushing weight of living at home was removed when she left for college, but there were many layers of healing she still needed to walk through: inviting community into her past pain, meeting her biological dad for the first time that she could remember, and letting God into the places that had been sealed shut, she thought, for her protection. She was, by the world's standards, abandoned, rejected, impoverished, abused, and the list goes on. But none of those designations were who she actually was. They were outside factors that, when not properly dealt with, attached themselves to her identity.

She later discovered that a lot of her stomach pains and other disorders were tied to her childhood trauma. After a lot of counseling, prayer, and healing, she was set free from the agony of her past. Fast-forward to today: Hannah is the most joyful, most healthy, and strongest person I know. If you were to meet her, you would never imagine she has gone through all those setbacks and devastating circumstances. Most people would have allowed those situations to become their identity, living the rest of their lives being depressed, searching for acceptance, and looking for anything to find worth in. Not Hannah. I asked her how she was able to maintain a positive sense of self amid so much pain and trauma. She said to me, bold and confident, "In the midst of all that darkness, I found my light. Those circumstances don't define me. I am wanted, chosen, and loved by God, and because of that, I know who I am."

When I look at Hannah's life, I see that we were never meant to be just the summation of the circumstances against us. No matter what labels other people have tried to put on you, you don't have to live by their designations. You can choose to break free and use your pain for a purpose. You can find a glimpse of hope and search for light in the midst of your darkness. You can choose to break free from the lies that make you ask, "Who am I?" **You are loved. You are enough. You are needed. That is who you are.**

Challenges on Identity

1. Be you. Normal is overrated. There are many pressures around us to be, look, and live a certain way, but my challenge to you is just to be you. Many voices surround you, but give careful thought to *whose* you listen to. You're more than enough. Stay true to who you are. God made you with unique gifts and traits. Celebrate who God made you to be. Look yourself in the mirror today and remind yourself of who you are. You are awesome!

2. Believe that you are who God says you are. You are not your circumstances. You are not what others have labeled you. You are not defined by your situations. And you are not limited by your circumstances—good or bad. Choose to believe that for yourself, and you will be able to rise in confidence and boldly declare, "I know who I am!"

3. Tune out the messages of this world that tell you what you should and shouldn't be. That could mean taking a break from social media for a week or a month or spending less time with people who don't love and accept who you are. Find people and activities that make you feel like your best self.

CHAPTER 8

THE COMPARISON KILLER

Grounding Yourself in Contentment

Who told you that you aren't pretty enough? Smart enough? Creative enough?

I would be willing to bet it's a big ole bully we all know. And its name is Comparison. Everyone deals with comparison. Everyone. But you don't have to let it kill your joy, your relationships, or your destiny.

As you now know, I was in a serious relationship for four years. I just knew this guy would be the one I would marry. But when that changed, I started wondering if I would ever find my guy. During the tortuous season after the breakup, it seemed like every one of my friends got engaged, married, and pregnant. As it turned out, I was asked to be in a lot of weddings. You know the saying: "Always the bridesmaid, never the bride." Well, it didn't take long for this feeling of exclusion to weigh heavy on my heart. I would see the rings. The *Say Yes to the Dress* real-life moments. The engagement posts. I would plan the bachelorette parties. One wedding after another. I was like, "Wait, God! I have done every-thing you asked me to do. I have been faithful and obedient. So why does it feel like everyone else is getting what I want? What about me!"

At one particular wedding, as I was getting dressed to attend the rehearsal dinner, I was suddenly struck with a daunting real-ization. In tears, I called my mom on the way to the dinner. I explained, "Mom! I am on my way to the rehearsal dinner and real-ized I will be sitting at the table with all the bridesmaids and their husbands. I am the *only* single one!" I was so distressed. My mom could hear the pain in my voice. I just knew she would tell me to turn the car around and call my friend to tell her I was sick. That would keep me from having to endure this dread of being alone, while all the couples enjoyed their dinner together. As couples. But instead, my pragmatic mother responded with, "Let me tell you something. You would rather sit at that table single than be sitting by the wrong husband. Don't compare your season with theirs. You definitely don't want it before you are ready for it." She continued to explain that while God was preparing me for what was coming, I had to keep my composure without comparing. She challenged me to use the pain I was feeling in the moment and turn it into purpose. She told me that what I would do during this season couldn't be done if I were married. What I would accomplish in the season of singleness would propel me forward and grow the impact I would have in the future. I listened.

I put on my highest heels, wiped my tears, picked up my head, and walked into that rehearsal dinner a little more confident. The room was filled with white roses and gold tinsel. The food smelled amazing. I may have been the only single one in the room, but I had the best time. The conversations during dinner had me laugh-ing so hard, I forgot that I was without a date. It ended up being a special night with incredible friends that comparison almost robbed me of.

I had to stop looking around the table at what others had and focus on what I had in order to live out my purpose and calling. It's hard to see who you are when you are too busy looking at who they are. It's hard to see what you have when you are too busy looking at what they have. It's hard to see where you are going when you are too busy looking at where they are going.

You have probably heard the saying "The grass is always greener on the other side." Often this mentality, derived from feelings of jealousy or insecurity, is due to an illusion. The jealous person doesn't usually see the valleys, the failures, the ups and downs "on the other side." People tend to zoom in on the brightest part of someone's journey, seeing an incomplete picture, missing the stages and steps that got that person where they are. When we focus on others, we lose important time that we could be investing in ourselves. Your grass will *never* become greener by comparing it with your neighbor's. Your grass becomes greener only when you value it by nurturing it and continually caring for it. Water your own grass and you won't have time to be jealous of other people's.

> When we focus on others, we lose important time that we could be investing in ourselves.

Social Media Lies

You know those people who seem to have it all—money, fame, perfect body, perfect life? Our envy toward these people is natural, but social media can magnify it. I often find myself scrolling through social media thinking thoughts like, "Wow! That girl has got it going on! How can she have perfect skin and hair, long gorgeous lashes, a goddess figure, and always be dressed to the nines?" It's difficult not to compare yourself when you constantly see photos of others at their best.

Have you noticed that people are experts at showcasing the best version of themselves? I love a quote by Pastor Steven Furtick: "One reason we deal with comparison is because we compare our behind the scenes to others' highlight reels."[1] Most people post only the best side of themselves—the high moments. We rarely see the troubles, the tough days, the low points. What we see on social media can create real comparison issues for us, but sometimes it's nothing more than an illusion. Sometimes behind those pictures is a person who drinks away their pain, takes pills to cope or to sleep, suffers from physical or mental pain and abuse, fights every night with a spouse or parent, or is drowning in debt. What we see is all smiles, white teeth, a new outfit, a perfectly filtered photo. And we think everything is perfect and we wish we were them. Sometimes we even overlook our own blessings, wishing we had what they pretend to have.

I can't tell you how many people who, by judging their social media posts, I thought had it all together. I envied their lives, only to find out after meeting them that they did not have it together, and they were not as perfect as I thought they were. In fact, many of them were in far worse situations than I was. Their struggles may have been different from mine, and they may have been in different seasons of life, but they were certainly not free from pain or disappointment.

We all have low points, insecurities, and internal battles. If we aren't careful, we allow social media to cause us to lose focus of who we are and what we have, which leads us to compare ourselves with others. We see friends eating lunch together, taking trips together, or showing off a display of gifts from each other. This can make us feel that our friendships don't measure up. We start to compare our lives with those of friends, and it looks like they are living it up, one amazing adventure after another. We see a friend post that her boyfriend sent her a dozen roses for no reason, and suddenly our boyfriend does not love us as much as hers. These types of comparisons can ruin relationships.

It seems we live in a world where followers and likes are proof of a person's worth, but **the number of followers, likes, or comments on social media does not determine your worth.**

Last fall I led a girls' small group at our local church. As we discussed life as a teenage girl, I realized these girls were living in a trap of comparison, and it was destroying their self-worth. When I asked the girls what they felt was the biggest contributor to their insecurities, they all said comparison and social media. One particular girl in the group shook me with her story. The following is Sophie's story.

I was so excited when I first started using social media. I got to post all my favorite pictures and got to see my friends' posts. I got to comment on their pictures and read all their comments on mine. It was so much fun. Until one day it wasn't fun anymore. Over time I started noticing that my friends were gaining more followers than I was. They were getting more likes than I was. And getting a lot more comments than I was. Comments about how great their bodies looked. Comments about how nice they dressed. Comments about how smart and athletic they were. Nobody commented these things on my page.

At first I was hurt. But then I started feeling depressed. I became obsessive over how much engagement my friends were getting and how little I was getting. I stopped wanting to go to school. I stopped wanting to go to parties or other social events. If people did not like me as much as they did everyone else, then I would just stay away from them. I started losing weight and became isolated. I didn't tell my family or my friends what was going on. I kept everything in. Hate. Bitterness. Resentment. Jealousy. I battled the realization that my insecurities and pain were self-inflicted. I knew the real underlying issue was much deeper than what was happening on social media. It was more about what I chose to believe about myself and how I let comparison with those girls affect how I felt about me. Social media just fed those anxieties and made them worse.

For over a year I was unhealthy—mentally, physically, and emotionally. I cried myself to sleep every night. I took diet pills and laxatives to try to lose weight. I started hanging out with different friends. Friends that were not a good influence. And then when I didn't think things could get any worse, they did. Someone left a comment under one of my photos that read, "You might want to take more diet pills." That was the last straw. I did take more of those pills. I took the whole bottle. It wasn't until after an attempted suicide that my family realized something was going on. They were able to get me the help I needed, and I am thankful to be alive today to tell my story.

I still use social media, and I still battle with insecurities. But I have learned how to focus more on my value and self-worth, my skills and abilities, and what makes me unique. What helped me most was taking a social media detox. I decided to do less scrolling and more living, to post less and do more. I realized that it didn't matter what others were doing; it mattered what I was doing. I stopped reading others' comments and stopped comparing who liked their post to who liked mine. It was time for me to refocus and create my own hashtag. I still have hard days, but I have tried to use what happened to me to help other girls who struggle with the same issue.

What bothers me most about Sophie's story is that she is just one of millions of girls who contend with comparison and low self-esteem. Millions of girls believe the lies that they do not measure up or that they are not enough because of the images they see on social media. Millions hide behind their pain and insecurities. They do everything they can to be seen or heard. To be accepted. Liked. Affirmed.

With social media playing such a big part in our lives, could we be sacrificing our mental health and well-being as well as our time? What does the evidence suggest? Here are a few facts I found when researching the negative effects of social media:

Two studies involving more than 700 students found that depressive symptoms, such as low mood and feelings of worthlessness and hopelessness, were linked to the quality of online interactions. Researchers found higher levels of depressive symptoms among those who reported having more negative interactions. . . .

A study of 1,000 Swedish Facebook users found that women who spent more time on Facebook reported feeling less happy and confident. The researchers concluded: "When Facebook users compare their own lives with others' seemingly more successful careers and happy relationships, they may feel that their own lives are less successful in comparison." . . .

In a study from 2013, researchers texted 79 participants five times a day for 14 days, asking them how they felt and how much they'd used Facebook since the last text. The more time people spent on the site, the worse they felt later on, and the more their life satisfaction declined over time. . . .

A study published in the *American Journal of Preventive Medicine* last year surveyed 7,000 19- to 32-year-olds and found that those who spend the most time on social media were twice as likely to report experiencing social isolation, which can include a lack of a sense of social belonging, engagement with others and fulfilling relationships.[2]

My prayer is that you will realize who you are and how much you are loved and that you will no longer allow social media to tell you anything different. Social media isn't all bad, but it is one of the biggest triggers for comparison. We have to kill comparison before it kills us. When the lies of comparison try to tell us what we are not, some practices can help us shift our minds to focus on contentment rather than comparison.

> We have to kill comparison before it kills us.

Be Grateful for What's Yours

Comparison can cause us to focus on the blessings in someone else's life while discounting or devaluing the blessings in our own lives. You might be satisfied with your life one day, and then comparison quickly leads you to think that your house isn't big enough, your car isn't new enough, your clothes aren't stylish enough, and your body isn't attractive enough. All those things are still what they were. Nothing changed. But when you compare those things with those of the girl standing beside you, their value suddenly decreases.

Until you are content with who you are and where you are on your journey, you will live in the trap of comparison and jealousy. You must learn to gain control of comparison tendencies if you want to achieve true happiness and success. Don't let comparison cause you to lose sight of the goodness in your own life. When you practice gratitude, you can appreciate what you have despite seeing what others have.

Most insecurity, jealousy, and discontentment is rooted in comparison. How many times have we asked the following questions: Why do things always seem to come easy for her? Why do people like her more than me? Why doesn't my boss appreciate me like he does her? Why does she always get chosen first, get called first, get the most likes? Why is everyone else married? Why is she always invited to all the big events? Why can't I ever be the favored one? Why is everyone else in a serious relationship? Why does her husband brag on her all the time?

These are all toxic questions. They lead to disappointment and dissatisfaction. I challenge you to say out loud or write down in your journal one thing you are grateful for each day. At first you might only be able to muster up the words, "I am grateful I'm breathing," but as days go by, you will find yourself looking for more ways to be grateful, and you will spend less time focusing on what you don't have. Comparison distracts you from your purpose. But there is power in choosing to be secure in who you are and grateful for all you have.

Celebrate Others' Successes

When we see others who are more successful and more talented than we are, we sometimes get jealous. Yet dragging others down will never make you rise higher. Rather, until you can celebrate the successes of others without comparing their successes to your own, you will never acquire your true potential. If you spend the majority of your time trying to outperform, outachieve, and outdo others, you will fall into a trap of comparison that will hinder your ability to be all God has called you to be and live a life of true fulfillment and purpose.

Can you be happy for someone else if God blesses them more than he blesses you? Craig Groeschel once said, "What if God is not blessing you like you want because you cannot celebrate the blessings in someone else's life?"[3] When we compare ourselves with others, it always diminishes our confidence. We often tell ourselves, "I'm not as pretty as she is," "I'm not as talented as they are," "I'm not as smart as she is." That's okay. We're not running their race. We don't need what they have. Let's admire other people's success, beauty, and happiness without questioning our own.

> Let's admire other people's success, beauty, and happiness without questioning our own.

Learn to celebrate others' successes instead of comparing yourself to them. Be quick to offer congratulations and high fives when others are successful. Comment on their post. Share it. Be proud of them. Be generous with your compliments. If you have a comparison thought toward someone for something they have achieved or obtained, go immediately to that person and congratulate them. Then go find ways to be successful yourself. Their success and blessing don't take away from yours. **Remember, her victory is not your loss. You have your own race to run.**

Focus on Your Lane

Whom do you need to stop comparing yourself with? For me, during my freshman year of basketball season, it was Jada. She had a jump shot that every basketball player dreamed of. You know the kind that causes the crowd to ooh and aah? It didn't matter how many extra hours I put in, I couldn't master the jump shot.

The more points Jada scored, the more I questioned my worth as a player on our team.

Until one day a fan came up to me and made a profound statement that changed my way of thinking. He said, "Very impressive game, Madi. Without your defense, assists, and ball-handling skills, there is no way we could have won that game." Boy, did my perspective change in that moment. I had been so focused on what Jada did well that I never gave myself credit for what I did well. I was so consumed with her successes and abilities that I failed to recognize my own. Rather than waste my time comparing myself to her, I needed to spend time maximizing my skills.

Looking enviously at other people's lanes only slows you down. Choose to let their success inspire you, not discourage you. Don't let envy rob you of all you have to offer. You won't find contentment in running other people's races; you'll find it when you fix your eyes on the lane in front of you and work to become the best you can be. Outperform yourself. Work harder and take greater pride in your own work. To find contentment, we need to keep our eyes straight ahead on the race marked out for us.

> Fix your eyes on the lane in front of you, and work to become the best you can be.

Remember—You Are Enough

God doesn't make mistakes. When he created you, he wasn't having an off day. He didn't randomly slap stuff together and say, "All right, this will work." No! He calls you his masterpiece. You have everything you need to fulfill your destiny. Stop comparing your looks, your success, your body, and your purpose. Be you. You are powerful. You are amazing. You are beautiful. You are gifted. You are one of a kind.

If you don't recognize that you are enough, you will always depend on other people to tell you who you are. You will market yourself to people, try to prove your worth, and even let them control you. That is where you will get your validation. But when you know you are enough by yourself, you won't rely on people to approve of you—you will get your approval from your heavenly Father. **The problem with relying on people for affirmation is that people can change.** If you feel good about yourself only when people validate you, then when they leave, you will forget who you are. But when you feel confident in who God made you, it doesn't matter what people do or don't do, if they show up or don't show up. You know you are a masterpiece all by yourself. You are *you*, and that is your power!

If a comparison thought enters your mind, recognize it, call it out, and don't let it enter your heart. Your purpose is far too important to be held back by the killer of comparison. Comparison can steal, kill, and ultimately destroy all that God has for us. Focusing on someone else and what they have will keep you from being everything God has called you to be. Instead, embrace who you are, and choose to live *your* best life, rather than pining after someone else's. To stop longing for greener grass and start being content with your own, practice being grateful for what you have, celebrating others' successes, and focusing on your lane. It's time to shrug off comparison and walk confidently in who God created you to be!

Challenges on Dealing with Comparison

1. Control social media instead of it controlling you. Your worth is not predicated by who follows you, likes your pictures, or calls you pretty on social media. Your identity and worth were given to you at birth, and no one can take those away from you. Try these practical tips to deal with social media struggles:
   - Notice when you compare yourself with others. Ask yourself, "Is this true? Does this line up with God's Word?" See if there is a pattern to what types of posts trigger those thoughts.
   - Once you note your social media triggers, set boundaries in place, such as limiting your time on social media, unfollowing certain people, or having friends or family hold you accountable.
   - Lastly, make sure the content you take in is life-giving. If you remove any stumbling blocks and you set proper boundaries, social media can be a place of great community and connection and a platform to encourage others.

2. Rest in contentment. Trust that what is meant for you will be yours. The moment you start celebrating the successes of others is the moment you will walk in freedom from comparison. Someone else's blessing is not your curse. Someone else's success is not your failure. Rest in contentment that you have what you need and you are who you are for a reason!

3. Believe that you are enough. You do not need anyone to validate your worth. Comparison distracts you from your purpose. But there is power in choosing to be secure in who you are and grateful for all you have.

CHAPTER 9

CONFIDENCE BOOST

Learning to Love Yourself
and Your Uniqueness

I ate a fish heart.

Yes, you read that right. On my second one-on-one date with Peter, we went fishing in Peru. As I pulled up to the scene, I was blown away by the beauty, culture, and uniqueness of this place! Every color you can imagine. Colorful boats, restaurants, and clothing. Kids running around laughing. Cute ice cream shops along the sidewalks. As I took in the beautiful culture around me, I was stopped and greeted with a smile and warm welcome by everyone who walked by. What a setting this was for a second date! Not to mention, it was a beautiful day, the perfect weather to catch some fish!

I didn't grow up fishing, but I was going to feign confidence in my ability to catch some fish. Confidence is everything, right? As I sat patiently waiting for a fishing pole to be handed to me, I was handed a block of wood with a string attached to it instead. I thought, "What kind of fishing is this? I don't know how to do this! Now I'm going to look silly instead of impressive and confident." The string was so long, and I had to unroll it off the block to get it to go down deeper in the water, for what felt like thirty minutes, just to get to the fish! I wasn't very good. My string kept getting tangled and caught on everything but the fish. I was getting frustrated that I couldn't catch anything.

Then it happened. I felt the tug! I just knew I was going to pull up a better fish than Peter. I pulled up my fish and I felt accomplished. I thought, "Great! What's next?" Little did I know that Peter wanted to cut up our caught fish and make our own ceviche. I looked at him like he grew ten heads. "I am sorry, what? You want me to slice open this fish that we just caught and eat it raw!" I am not much of a raw meat or fish kind of gal. I am pretty picky with the food I eat. I eat like a girl born and raised in the South, with a basic diet of fried chicken, hot dogs, and pizza. What else do you need?

However, you should know that I never back down from a challenge. But this? I was already feeling a little seasick, and now cutting into a fish and eating it on the boat? Oh, I was sure to puke everywhere—how attractive. Peter and I started gutting the fish. Once we cut the fish into little pieces, we put it into a bowl with citrus juices and spices and mixed it all together. I could feel my stomach twisting and turning. I tried my best to hold it in.

Somehow I was able to convince myself that I was not sick. The ceviche wasn't bad—the lime juice and seasonings helped. Apparently, the dish is common in Peru, where ceviche first originated. I guess I couldn't call myself a Peru native quite yet. Just as I thought we were done and ready to head back from this wild date, Peter looked at me and said, "It's time for us to give each other our hearts." I thought he was being sweet. I thought, "This guy! He's about to tell me he loves me." Not exactly. I looked down and he was holding the fish heart. I almost threw up just looking at it. He went on to divide it in half, suggesting we each eat half the heart. "What is happening? Who does this? Am I being pranked?" Again, I am not one to back down from a challenge, so I tried not to think about what I was doing and threw back the fish heart and swallowed it fast, immediately chasing it down with water. It left the worst gritty feeling on my tongue. It was so gross. Peter looked at me with a regretful look on his face and said, "Madi, I'm not even sure if that was the heart." I'm sorry, what! We laughed for a good ten minutes straight as we both tried not to think about what we might have possibly just digested. Although this part of the date wasn't aired for everyone to see, our gross and funny moment of eating fish guts will be forever engrained in my memory.

This is what God wants for you. Not eating a fish heart, of course. But for you to give him your whole heart—jokes aside. Only by doing this will you discover your true identity and purpose. Only through discovering who you truly are can you walk in confidence in who you were created and destined to be.

When you're a confident woman, you not only know who you are but also don't have to prove your worth. Unlike me in this story of trying to impress Peter with catching the fish and eating a raw fish heart, when you are confident and know what you bring to the table and how valuable you are, you don't feel the need to perform to be accepted or loved. **Your value comes from what is inside you, not from what you can do.**

What Is Confidence?

Where does confidence come from? What do you put your confidence in? Many have misidentified what confidence is and where it is found. For us to truly discover what confidence is, we must first confront what confidence is not.

Confidence is not:

- a feeling or emotion
- an action
- a personality trait
- circumstantial
- found in self
- fitting the perfect "beauty standard"
- increased or decreased by your job, social media following, or upbringing

Many of us have misplaced our confidence. We have placed it in people, accomplishments, approval, and so much more. Do any of those sound familiar to you? Ask yourself, "When do I feel most confident? When do I feel most insecure?" If we are being honest with ourselves, we probably associate our good moments with winning or accomplishing something, or feeling like we looked good and someone noticed, or being wanted and pursued by others. And we associate our bad moments with, well, the opposite. The thing is, if we depend on people and circumstances as the source of our confidence, what happens when they change? When they fail us? Our confidence is shattered. The good news is that there is a way to be confident no matter what someone says about you, whether you win or lose, or whether you are accepted or rejected.

True confidence, the kind we all want and hope for, is created by God and sustained through him. That means that confidence is available to all of us, yet it is up to us to receive it and embrace it. That is the difference between God-confidence and self-confidence. If God is the source, it is sustained through him. If we are the source, or other people are the source, it has to be sustained through us. God is perfect and he will never fail us. If producing and sustaining our confidence is up to us, it is sure to spiral out of control and come crashing down.

> True confidence, the kind we all want and hope for, is created by God.

As we read in chapter 7, it is God's Word that tells us who we are. But it is the Spirit of God inside us that develops the confidence we need to walk in that identity daily. God wants all of us to live confident, abundant lives, yet many of us never break through our own walls of doubt, fear, and insecurity to seek out the kind of life that was ours all along. In Lisa Bevere's book *Girls with Swords*, she reminds us that "our hero status is not dependent on our human might or power or even our human spirit; it comes from the power of his Spirit."[1]

Steven Furtick says it this way: "True confidence is a by-product of belonging."[2] As you become more confident in the God who created you and saved you, you will grow more confident in his creation—*you!* When you know, truly know, who you belong to, you will be confident in who you are. Confidence is built when you partner with God, knowing you aren't enough on your own but you are more than enough with him. It's time to stop trying to do it all on your own and start trusting and believing in who God is and in who he says you are.

The same Jesus who was mocked, beaten, and crucified for me was for you too. As he hung on the cross, he thought about you. You were worth everything to him, even death on a cross. If you are worth it to the God of this universe, who cares if others stand in agreement? Your worth isn't determined by them. God doesn't rank us as the world does. He doesn't view some as better than others. He views you just as he views me: his beloved child.

I don't care what your past looks like, how bad your current circumstances are, or what other people believe or don't believe about you—you belong! Not because of who you are but because of who God is. Not because of what you can or can't do but because of what was already done for you.

God doesn't rank us as the world does. He views you as his beloved child.

For so long I lacked confidence; I felt that I had to perform and work hard to get approval from others to be accepted and loved. If only I did my makeup a little better, or made a funnier comeback, or studied harder to get better grades, or practiced longer to be the best athlete, or took better pictures for Instagram to get more likes, or made a little more money to buy name-brand clothes—then I would be confident. My confidence was always contingent on something, so it always fluctuated, especially in relationships. I would give anything to hear, "I love you." I would find myself performing just to hear those words, working for love as if it were something to be earned.

I love you—the three words we all long to hear. We date someone for months, waiting on the edge of our seat to hear those three powerful words. Why? Because our greatest desire in the world is to love and to be loved. Hearing those words brings a certain blanket of security and wave of confidence. We know where we stand with that person. No more tearing off flower petals, hoping the last petal lands on "he loves me." No more asking his friends how he feels or trying to analyze his every move. Those words let us know exactly how he feels and where he stands.

Why does loving someone else seem easier than loving ourselves? Sadly, most of us don't know how to love ourselves. We have been taught that self-love comes in the form of shopping sprees, spa days, and Instagram-worthy posts. If you're supposed to love yourself, how do you do that? Do you know what that even means? If it isn't buying fancy clothes, treating yourself to a box of warm donuts, and sitting in a hot tub until your fingers are wrinkly, then what is it?

Many of us struggle with confidence because we don't really like ourselves. We can't stand to spend time with ourselves or even look ourselves in the mirror. We wouldn't even know where to start with loving ourselves. We are ashamed of how we look, the mistakes we've made, and who we believe we are. We long for the day we can love ourselves but don't know how to begin. Let's talk about realistic steps we can take to start the self-love journey.

Loving yourself starts with treating yourself as someone you love. Think about it. How much time, money, and attention do we spend on someone we love? We spend hours looking for the right dress to impress them, studying what interests them, and writing letters or leaving little gifts, going the extra mile with our words and actions to let them know how we feel about them and what they mean to us. So why is it so difficult for us to do that for ourselves? Why are we quick to affirm, encourage, and love others, but not ourselves?

Matthew 22:39 says, "Love your neighbor as yourself." It clearly declares that we won't be able to love others until we learn to love ourselves. This is huge. We are called to have relationships, but we can't truly enjoy these relationships, loving fully and receiving freely, until we learn to love ourselves. Many of us have heard this idea before but never truly taken time to think about it.

The first step to loving yourself is embracing who you are right now. Ask yourself, "Who am I right now?" I don't mean who others want you to be or who you hope to become, but who you are right now. Include the messy, broken, and beautiful parts that make you *you*. Just as you put in the time to get to know someone you're dating, you should put in the quality time to get to know yourself. Have you spent time doing that? Why not try it? Dating yourself, getting to know the real you—what makes you all that you are, how you respond to certain situations, what makes you happy and what makes you angry—will help you love yourself better. You might think I'm crazy for suggesting that you should date yourself. But think about it. In a relationship, the only way you can truly love that person is to know them well by spending time with them and embracing them for who they are and who they are becoming. And we should know ourselves better than anyone else knows us.

The second step to loving yourself is avoiding negative self-talk. For some reason, a lot of women bond over tearing themselves down. They say things like, "Oh my gosh, look how big I am!" "My hair looks so ugly today," "I am so stupid!" "I am so out of shape." But we sometimes don't realize that our words carry weight. The more we speak these negative remarks over ourselves, the more we continue to believe them. For me, sometimes it helps to speak the opposite of what I feel. When I wake up and feel ugly, I try to look myself in the mirror and say, "You look beautiful and you are beautiful." When I feel unwanted or rejected, I write a Bible verse on my hand that reminds me that I am chosen, wanted, and loved. Or when I am in a hard season, when all my friends are married and I am the only single one, or when everyone else is getting the opportunities, I write on my mirror in bold letters, "You are enough. You have purpose. You are not alone. You are loved."

Now ask yourself, "Who do I want to be?" Remember, words have power, producing life or death. What are your words producing? **Be careful which words follow your "I am."**

The third step is to start small but strategic. Have a goal of where you want to be and who you want to become. Then make a plan for how to get there. But understand that like anything worthwhile in life, building confidence and loving yourself well takes time, patience, and consistency. Most times these qualities are developed through being consistent with the small things. The last question I want you to ask yourself is, "How do I become that person?" Remember, it is the small steps that lead to great change. "I love this quote that captures the philosophy of Aristotle: "We are what we repeatedly do."[3] So what are you repeating every day? Are you consistent and repetitive with the small things and doing them well?

Over time, through taking these three steps, you will no longer operate from a place of lack, looking and waiting for others to complete you and love you. Instead, you'll feel whole, loving and accepting yourself, and in turn you'll have a healthy love to give to others. **You will begin to see yourself as beautiful, destined, worthy, and valuable, and you won't feel the need to change for anyone else. You will begin to walk in confidence and embrace who you are. Why? Because you know God loves you, and so you love you.**

What Takes Away Confidence?

Football is not my sport.

I am sure by this point you have picked up on the fact that I am very competitive. I hate losing. While on *The Bachelor,* I hoped to land one of the dates where I could show off my athletic skills. I wanted some good, healthy competition. The first couple of weeks, I didn't go on any of the group dates since I went on the first one-on-one date. Our first destination once we left the mansion was Cleveland, Ohio. I thought, "This is my time to shine!" I knew the dates would be centered on sports since the city is home to the

NBA Cavaliers and the NFL Browns. When the date card arrived, because of the clues, we all knew the group date had something to do with sports, but we weren't sure which one. I had never played football, other than messing around with friends, but I knew my athleticism and competitiveness would secure me a win.

I woke up that morning so excited for the date, but when I took a look in the mirror, I saw what no girl wants to see: a pimple the size of Mars on my face! I could've started my own galaxy with what was happening on my chin. It was tragic. It wasn't like when girls say, "My skin is breaking out so bad," but you would have to get out a magnifying glass to find the pimple. No. This pimple was noticeable from miles away. I tried my best to cover it up with makeup, but even that couldn't cover this monster.

We showed up to the Browns stadium—football it is. The girls were going to play football against each other to win time with Peter. As we were warming up and stretching, it started pouring rain. Oh, great. All that makeup to cover up this pimple, and it washed right off. I was not in my element, to say the least. We went into the locker room to get ready for the game. We had our pep talk and drew up plays. We put our mouth guards in, slapped one another on the butt, and hit each other's helmets. Now we were ready to go.

A song came on and smoke filled the tunnel. I felt like I was on an episode of *Friday Night Lights*. We ran out in the still-pouring rain. We were a bunch of girls acting like we were Division I athletes. We lined up to take our positions and called out our play. As soon as Sydney, our quarterback, said the magic words, I went long. When I started running, I quickly realized that my helmet didn't fit. It bounced back and forth, covering my face and eyes. I didn't give up; I hoped maybe we would have some crazy intuition. My foot slipped and I fell flat on my face. Great. First play of the game, and already it wasn't looking good. Next play, same thing: my helmet covered my face, and I missed the ball. Okay, so we needed to come up with another game plan. Get the ball to Shiann. She scored. Hope was returned! My tiny, pea-sized head wasn't going to add much value, so I focused on what I could control: defense. All I had to do was tackle and not let them score. Easy. Not so much. Even that was hard with the wet grass and loose helmet.

The fourth quarter came fast, and it had been back and forth. The score was tied. Sydney handed off the ball to Shiann, and she scored again! With not much time left in the game, we assumed we had this in the bag! As we were leaving the huddle to go line up, the other team hiked the ball and ran down and scored. I thought, "What? That's unfair! We weren't ready." The referee didn't do anything about it. Time ran out and the game was called in a tie. My mouth dropped, and before I knew it, I was arguing, "That's not how it works! There is a winner and a loser!" Later I was so embarrassed by how mad I was that the game ended in a tie.

The next day I woke up so sore, barely able to walk or move, with tons of bruises covering my body. I reflected on the date, my attitude, and how I handled everything. I journaled and thought about how I was putting too much confidence and hope in myself. From how I looked, to how I played, to how I handled myself—it was clear that because I didn't look my best or perform my best, I felt insecure and angry. I lacked confidence. I got caught up in what I looked like and winning a football game. I had to remind myself that I have more to offer than just my body, my face, and my scoring ability. The most beautiful thing I have to offer is my spirit, and that was what I really wanted Peter to be attracted to.

I know that is a silly story, but don't we all do this? When we place our confidence in how we perform and whether people accept and appreciate that effort, it constantly rises and falls, like a roller coaster. Instead, we should be steady under pressure, knowing that whatever approaches us, we can handle it. Our confidence shouldn't be predicated on outside circumstances—if the weather is good, if our skin is clear, if we can fit into a certain size shorts, if everyone loves us, if we always get the perfect grade. It should come from within, holding firm no matter what is happening around us. The most confident people I have met aren't the ones who have everything or lead an easy life, but the ones who know who they are and that they are a part of something bigger than themselves.

We often allow circumstances, feelings, and other people to determine how we feel about ourselves. Aren't you tired of feeling insecure, discontent, and disappointed? A lot of us have grown up hearing, "Be confident in yourself! Pick your head up. Self-confidence is everything." I want to offer a different perspective. Confidence is important, but it doesn't come from yourself.

As we talked about earlier, there is a huge difference between self-confidence and God-confidence. Self-confidence puts energy and value in what you wear, how you look, and how much other people like and value what you are putting out there. God-confidence is about giving your best in all you do but knowing that true value comes from the One who creates and gives it.

> Until you know your value and respect yourself, you can't expect someone else to value and respect you.

Girl, I'll let you in on a little secret. Confidence is attractive! When you're a confident woman, you don't have to prove your worth to anyone. You don't have to perform to be accepted or loved. Your worth isn't based on a performance or increased by the validation or affirmation of other people. Until you know your value and respect yourself, you can't expect someone else to value and respect you. A lot of things try to rob us of our confidence. To win in confidence, we need to know what we are fighting against.

- **Comparison.** As we discussed earlier, when we compare ourselves with others, we are seeing only the surface of their lives, not the full reality. God has given you unique passions, talents, and gifts for what he has purposed you to do. When you use your energy and emotion to focus on what you don't have, it's almost as if you are telling God that he didn't get it right. Friend, God doesn't make mistakes. He has given you grace for your race, not for hers. No matter how hard you try, you won't be able to do it like she does it. You weren't meant to. Focus on your race!
- **Fear.** Fear is one of the biggest reasons many lack confidence. Fear produces negative thoughts, causing us to jump to the worst possible scenarios or conclusions. It often holds our minds in an invisible prison cell, yet we are the only ones who hold the keys to free ourselves. Fear keeps us from truly living and being all God has called us to be. Throughout God's Word there are at least 365 references to fear in the Bible. I don't believe that is a coincidence. God knew we would face fear; that's why he has given us an encouraging reminder for every day of the year!
- **Body image.** "Approximately 91% of women are unhappy with their bodies."[4] Let me start off by saying that taking care of your body and pursuing a healthy lifestyle is important, for God's Word tells us that our bodies are temples of the Holy Spirit (1 Corinthians 6:19). But your value doesn't come from what you look like and whether others think you fit the perfect "beauty standard." The most valuable thing you have

is your spirit. Make sure that is what you invest the most time in. When we dress a certain way, do certain things to our bodies, and flaunt what we have to get people's attention, all that does is feed our ego for a moment, but it leaves us wanting. Yet when we invest in our spirit and feed it with God's Word; healthy, life-giving friendships; and prayer and worship, we don't seek validation for our outward appearance.

- **Pressures from mainstream media.** Research tells us that "students, especially women, who consume more mainstream media, place a greater importance on sexiness and overall appearance than those who do not consume as much."[5] The sad fact is that as women, we are pressured by the media to believe the lies that beauty looks a certain way, love looks a certain way, and success looks a certain way. It hurts me that so many women buy into these lies and give into these pressures. If media affects you to the point of harming yourself, questioning your worth or beauty, being anxious or depressed, or changing yourself to fit the "standard," I encourage you to make some changes where social media is concerned, as we talked about in chapter 8.

- **Failures or unmet expectations.** Often we equate God's goodness and faithfulness to our experiences with people. When people meet our expectations and treat us the right way, we see God as good; when they don't, we see God as unfaithful, letting us down. We ask, "God, how could you let them do this to me? I thought you loved me." We have to stop dumbing God down to our level. God's ways are higher and greater than we could ever comprehend. We are going to experience troubles, some turbulence along the way, but we can rest in confidence that God will always work them out for our good (Romans 8:28).

- **Past mistakes or traumas.** Many of us have been through tough breaks, losses, breakups, and bad days. Some of us have even experienced abuse or violence. Whatever your trauma or pain has been, I am heartbroken for you. But I don't want your past to rob you of the life God has for you. I believe in a God that loves us and is for us. Yet there is also a very real Enemy, who is against us and wants to see us suffer and drown in sorrow for the rest of our lives. But what the Enemy means for harm God will turn around and use it for good (Genesis 50:20). He can take your broken heart and mend it back together and use it in a way you never could've imagined. He can take your pain and use it for a greater purpose—the saving of many lives. Keep hoping, pressing in, and trusting that God is for you, and he will use whatever you have been through for a divine purpose.

Many things, all around us, try to steal our confidence. We must be intentional about what voices we listen to and how we invest our time. We have to stop letting our feelings and emotions lead our lives. Standing on the truth of God's Word, we need to have the self-control and courage to take our lives back and make choices that will keep us grounded and rooted in God's Word so we can live the abundant life God has for us.

How to Boost Your Confidence

There are many things that can take away from our confidence, but the good news is that there are many steps we can take to boost our confidence! The secret to boosting confidence is intentional living. Ask yourself when you have decisions to make, "Does this push me closer to Jesus or away from him?" or, "Does this feed my spirit or hurt my spirit?" Let's take a look at some practical steps that can help us live intentionally.

1. **Memorize Scripture and pray it over yourself daily.** Whatever area you find yourself struggling in, whether it is fear, comparison, or lack of purpose, find two or three verses that speak life and truth over that area, and cling to them. When life gets hard and your feelings speak louder than your heart and mind, God's Word will keep you anchored. Say these words: *Because I am in Christ, I am loved.*

    Romans 5:8 says, "God demonstrates his own love for us in this: While we were still sinners, Christ died for us."

2. **Believe in who God says you are.** One way to grow your confidence is to grow in belief of who God is. The more confident you are in God's sovereignty, the more confident you will be in you. I know that sounds almost too basic to be included as a practical step, but that belief gets you from head knowledge to heart change. All day long you can read, hear, or watch messages that preach, "God loves you. You are his beloved, and in him you have belonging. God is with you—you are not alone." But until you believe it for yourself, nothing will change. No one can force you to be confident or make you believe the truth of who you really are. Only you can choose what you believe. Say these words with me: *Because I am in Christ, I am secure.*

    Isaiah 54:10 says,

    > "Though the mountains be shaken
    >   and the hills be removed,
    > yet my unfailing love for you will not be shaken
    >   nor my covenant of peace be removed,"
    >   says the LORD, who has compassion on you.

3. **Embrace the process.** Growing your confidence doesn't happen in a day. It is a process. It involves everyday decisions and discipline. Learn to accept that what has happened around you, to you, and because of you does not define you. Even after the mistakes you've made, choose to believe you are not one. Even with everything you have been through, know that you have purpose. Be encouraged that your obedience to walk in confidence may even have a positive effect on someone else's destiny and eternity. Say these words with me: *Because I am in Christ, I am significant.*

   Matthew 10:31 says, "Don't be afraid; you are worth more than many sparrows."

4. **Develop intentional relationships.** The most important and intentional relationship you should have is with God. After that, choose whom you surround yourself with. Remember, confidence doesn't come from a person, yet the people around us do have an impact on whether that confidence is boosted or hindered. Unfortunately, I have seen many amazing women never reach their full potential because of the company they kept. Our time on this earth is short; don't waste it with the wrong people by your side. Be intentional with your relationships!

5. **Foster intentional service.** The fastest way to boost your confidence is to take what God has given you and use it to serve someone else. It's a win-win: you help someone, and you grow in confidence as you see your gifts and passions bless that person! This is what we were created to do: add value to people and make a difference. Find ways to serve those around you.

It's time to identify the person you want to be and commit to intentionally becoming all you were meant to be. To be ready for life's toughest blows and defining moments, you need to know who you are and walk in that confidence. It isn't always easy, nor will you always feel like doing it, but your level of confidence is directly tied to your level of intentionality. I would like to tell you that if you decide today, "I'm going to be confident!" then all your insecure thoughts will disappear for good, but that isn't exactly how it works. Yet in being intentional with your daily choices in everyday moments, you will begin to see that confidence boost you have been waiting for!

> Your level of confidence is directly tied to your level of intentionality.

Challenges on Confidence

1. Love yourself. As we talked about in this chapter, ask yourself, "Who am I right now?" Right now, pull out your journal and write down this question along with your answer (and be honest!) Confidence begins with loving yourself. And you can't love someone you don't know, so take time to get to know yourself. Study your passions, dreams, gifts, and weaknesses. Reflect on your past, and write out your dreams for your future. Take yourself on some dates—sometimes a little TLC from you and for you is all you need!

2. Embrace your uniqueness and value it. Now write down, "Who do I want to be?" and answer that question. You weren't meant to be like anyone else. Therefore, you shouldn't have to change who you are or prove yourself to anyone. A confident woman knows that through the highs and lows of life, she is full of purpose and fully known and deeply loved by her Creator and Savior.

3. Live intentionally so you can live a life you are proud of. Ask yourself, "How do I become the person I want to be?" and write out your answer. Then write out intentional disciplines you want to implement to become that person you long to be. That could mean cutting out one unhealthy food group or unfollowing certain social media accounts. Maybe you need to memorize one Bible verse a day or go on walks in your neighborhood. Maybe you need to leave notes to remind yourself of how awesome you are. When your confidence is in God, you will become secure, fulfilled, consistent, and at peace as you walk out your purpose and begin making a difference in the world around you.

CHAPTER 10

CHECK YOUR SURROUNDINGS

How the Company You Keep Influences Your Character

One thing you should know about me: I have always had poor vision, or at least I used to. I recently had LASIK surgery, and now I can see 20/20. Praise God! Anyway, before then, I tried many types of contacts, but my eyes were so sensitive, and I could wear contacts for only a little over an hour before they would start to torture my eyes, and I hated wearing my glasses. So I was constantly squinting my eyes and was known as the girl who couldn't see anything. I have many embarrassing and funny stories because of not being able to see, but this one takes the cake.

Another thing you should know about me: I don't wear heels. Like, ever. I prefer my feet to be comfortable, and I love the look of a clean pair of sneakers. So you can usually catch me in my Jordans.

When I was on *The Bachelor*, everyone joked with me and gave me a hard time when we had to wear heels. The rose ceremonies were once a week, and we were encouraged to wear our dresses and heels. About thirty minutes into the night, I would be limping or tripping. They all laughed, knowing I couldn't walk in heels, and we all waited for the moment I would face-plant on national television. Even the first night, I walked out in my evening gown with my Jordans on underneath. My point is: I only wear sneakers.

I'm not sure what was going through my mind, but for my senior prom, I decided to wear stilettos. Each year, the prom had a theme, and that year was a *Great Gatsby* theme. The classy, rich, 1920s vibe—got to love it! We spent hours planning and decorating, and everything came together beautifully. We did F. Scott Fitzgerald and Leonardo DiCaprio proud.

To start off the night, the senior class was introduced. My date and I lined up and got ready to walk down the stairs to strut our stuff as soon as our names were called. I peeked out behind the curtain that blocked us off from the crowd. Parents, staff, and other students filled the dance room floor, with cameras and phones ready to capture the moment! I had already started joking with my date about how I couldn't wait to sit down and take off my shoes and start dancing. Because we were being called alphabetically, my feet were starting to kill me! Couldn't they hurry up and get to *P* already?

They finally called our names. We started walking down the stairs, and suddenly all the stairs looked like they were blending together. While attempting to walk gracefully, looking back and forth between the stairs and the cameras, all with a smile on my face, I missed two whole steps and fell face forward toward the ground. My date almost came crashing down with me but caught his balance just in time. The whole crowd gasped. I knew I could either let this fall ruin my night or play it off all cool-like.

So I jumped up, put both hands in the air, and said, "Let's get this party started!" Then I had to keep walking down the red carpet they had laid out below the stairs, with everyone still staring at me with pity and secondhand embarrassment. We finally got to the end of the red carpet, and my date and I started dying laughing. He asked me what happened and how I missed the steps. I said, "For starters, I can't see a thing, and second, I can't walk in heels. But I guess I didn't check my surroundings well enough." Now it makes for a laughable and memorable story. Thankfully, I don't get embarrassed easily, and I didn't let it ruin my senior prom. If anything, it was a warm-up for all the dancing I was about to do!

If I had done a better job of checking my surroundings, I wouldn't have fallen. I think we often find ourselves flat on the ground, forgetting how we got there, and then we're so low we don't know how to get back up. Our poor decisions can lead us to rock bottom, looking for a hand to help us up. Our surroundings sometimes influence our character. And negative influences and bad environments usually lead us to make poor choices. I want to help you so that you don't have to fall like I did! Or even if you have, we can get up together. To become who we want to be in moments of pressure, we need to be selective of the company we keep, make sure to walk with the wise, and put ourselves in environments that help us grow.

The Company You Keep

At prom, the cost of not checking my surroundings ended up being pretty laughable. But other times the cost has been much more serious.

At the beginning of high school, one of my best friends moved to a new school. So I started hanging with a new group of friends. They were popular and fun, and everyone wanted to be a part of their friend group. One night, one of the girls in the group wanted to prank another girl at our school because she had taken her spot as cheer captain. She had been ranting about her all night, and so it was decided: we were going to toilet-paper the girl's car. I thought, "No big deal. It's just toilet paper!"

We got the supplies and were ready to go. Some heavy drinking was going on around me, and feeling the pressure, I drank too. It was my first time drinking, and it didn't take much to feel a little "off the wall."

We had planned only to toilet-paper her car, but that wasn't all that happened. The guys egged her car, and the girls wrote mean things on her car windows. I tried my best to sit off to the side, just watching, but one of the girls came up and handed me an egg to throw at the girl's bedroom window. I thought, "If I say no, they'll think I'm a coward and I'll be seen as uncool. If I say yes, I'll be participating in harassing this girl." The guys started chanting and proceeded to count down. Giving in, I took a few big gulps of a drink, grabbed an egg, and launched it at her bedroom window. After seeing the lights flicker on, we all bolted.

I felt so guilty all night, but I didn't tell anyone what we'd done. We had promised each other we wouldn't snitch. But the next day at school, it was the biggest hot gossip. Word spread fast, and the girl's family got the police involved. I was so nervous, I felt like I was going to have a heart attack. I thought, "If I get questioned, I am the world's worst liar!" I also knew if my dad found out, he would ground me for life. There was talk that the police were going to the house after school to fingerprint the empty paint markers that were left on the ground. I knew I needed to come clean or I could get into serious trouble.

As soon as I got home from school, I told my parents. They were so upset and disappointed in me, which to me is much worse than if they were angry. I hate disappointing my parents. They made me go to the girl's house to apologize to her and her family. It was brutal. I took the full blame for everything because I didn't want anyone else to get in trouble.

After that crazy experience and weeks of being grounded, I reflected on the situation. I had compromised my convictions and character, and I was usually pretty firm in my convictions. What caused me to stray? What influenced my decisions that night? The company I was with.

Hear me out: I'm not blaming my choices on other people, because no one forced me to do anything. No one forced me to hang out with them or throw that egg at the girl's window. I still made those decisions for myself. But I was becoming like those I surrounded myself with. They were influencing my choices. I had compromised and done things I wouldn't usually do (like egg a girl's car!)

That was a revelation moment. I knew the kind of person I wanted to be and who I truly was deep down. I knew I needed to make a change. I needed to put some healthy distance between me and those who made me feel conflicted about my actions when I was with them. So I decided to make a shift. I became more selective about people I spent time with. I started to hang around with people who saw greatness inside me and wanted to help pull that out of me. Friends who I could be myself around and who made me laugh. Friends who saw every bit of potential inside me and loved me for who I was and who I was becoming.

When I finally hit pause to check my surroundings, it made all the difference.

The cold, hard truth is, in the heat of the moment, you'll feel pressure and the desire to fit in or the hope to be accepted. This is natural, but there is much to be gained by taking a beat and not letting reactivity get the best of you. Obviously, I am not always perfect at this. Just as in this story of drinking and egging a girl's house, often I have given in to those emotions and pressures. **Yet I have discovered that when I have the right company around me, it is much easier to stand firm in who I am, to be led by conviction over feeling, and to respond with wisdom and grace instead of emotion.**

So, I ask you, what does your circle look like? What kind of company do you keep? Have you checked your surroundings lately? Those moments when you made decisions you feel guilty about—was it because of who you were with? I'm going to guess that 98 percent of the time that's a yes. Usually it's a friendship or relationship that causes you to compromise or become complacent. So take a look at your circle and make the necessary changes so that you can be ready for your God-given moments!

I always told my younger sisters the two most important statements I could challenge them with: know who you are, and then choose carefully whom you want to do life with. You will become like those you surround yourself with. Show me your circle of friends, and I can tell you who you are becoming and what your future will look like. So, girl, it's time to check your surroundings.

Maybe you have a lot of friends, but they aren't making you better, encouraging you, and challenging you to be your best. Or maybe you don't have anyone around you, and you feel all alone. Or maybe those around you are bringing you down. You now find yourself doing things you didn't do before, compromising in areas you said you never would, becoming complacent in your everyday life, and cruising through life with no ambition, motivation, or tenacity. I'm not judging you; trust me, I have been in every one of those places. That is why I am challenging you and encouraging you to find friends who see greatness within you and who will push you to higher heights. Your strongest relationships will either help or hinder your desired future.

The Bible tells us in Proverbs 27:17, "As iron sharpens iron, so one person sharpens another," which insinuates that both parties have to be strong enough to sharpen the other. If you have a piece of iron and a piece of glass, one is fragile and weak and one is strong; they can't sharpen each other. You both have to be strong and stable to sharpen each other and make each other better. The only way iron gets sharper is for it to be sharpened by its own kind, iron.

> Your strongest relationships will either help or hinder your desired future.

For you to get better and stronger, you need iron around you. I choose my close circle wisely. I have three to four close friends I allow to walk alongside me and come into the sacred spaces in my heart.

Your life, your heart, and your future are all important and should be treated with respect and value. If you don't value them, who will? If your strongest relationships help or hinder your desired future, then choose the right people to walk alongside you.

If you want to be successful in life, you must surround yourself with winners. If you want to be a trend-setter, surround yourself with innovators. If you want to do something that has never been done before, surround yourself with pioneers, visionaries, and dreamers. If you want to be the best, you have to surround yourself with the best.

Surround yourself with positive people who lift you higher. People who speak life. People who are confident and lead themselves well. People you would want to become. You may need to face your own tendency to feel "less than" others and learn what it means to surround yourself with "more than" kind of people!

The people in your life will either inspire you or drain you. Choose carefully. You have to be willing to walk away from those who drag you down. You will never see a successful person hanging around a dream killer. Find and activate courage within to remove the negative people from your life. In doing this, you will see your energy and enthusiasm blossom.

The people in your life will either inspire you or drain you.

Letting go of the relationships that aren't bettering you is an important step if you want to become more positive, fulfilled, and purposeful. Detoxing your life from negative influences also allows you to become the person you truly hope to be. You'll free yourself from the constant complaining, meaningless conversations, and criticism.

Take a look at the people around you, and ask yourself these three questions:

- Do my friends speak life to me or discouragement?
- When I spend time with my friends, do I leave feeling empowered to be better, or do I find myself being pulled down or fighting the temptation of mediocrity or even negativity?
- If I were to become the average of my three closest friends, would I be happy with who I have become?

Walk with the Wise

During my last few weeks on *The Bachelor,* feelings of fear and anxiety constantly swirled through my thoughts, and not having my friends and family around to help me make big decisions was getting harder and harder. Have you ever felt that lump in your throat—the kind that stays there when you are really nervous? Let's just say that lump never really went away the last two weeks I was on the show. I felt like there was so much at stake, and I felt so alone. But after forty days without talking to my family, I was relieved that the day had finally arrived: hometowns. Hometown dates are for the last four girls remaining on the show. They invite the Bachelor to their hometowns to meet their families and see where they grew up.

When Peter arrived in Auburn, I was able to show him around all my favorite spots, especially the Auburn basketball arena. I showed off some of my mad basketball skills. He was majorly impressed. Peter attempted to show me some of his dribbling skills, but it resulted more in laughter than competition. It was so fun.

Then it was time for Peter to meet my family! He would finally see me surrounded by my people. So many thoughts went through my head. I couldn't wait to see them, but I wondered, "Will they like him? Will they approve?" I had always gone to my parents for wisdom, advice, and direction. Not being able to get their insight for forty days had been brutal. I didn't know what to expect, and I couldn't wait to hug them.

When Peter and I arrived at my parents' house, I was a little nervous. But as soon as I saw my parents, my fear started to dissipate. The evening was full of sweet tea, hard questions, long hugs, and a lot of tears.

This night brought a lot into perspective for me. I have always valued the wisdom and advice of those older than me, especially my parents. I knew the conversations that night wouldn't be easy. I knew my parents would challenge me and test our relationship to see if it was grounded, unshakable, and rooted in the right things. When the night ended, leaving my parents was hard; I didn't want to separate from them again, especially when I knew I had big decisions to make. I had a week before I would see Peter again for the next rose ceremony. I knew I needed to take the week to pray about everything I had talked about with my parents.

Often in life it's easy to do whatever feels good or is easy or convenient. We like to stay in our comfort zones, and opening ourselves up to challenges is hard because sometimes that means our comfort, expectations, hopes, and dreams are questioned. It would have been easy to be shut off to my parents' feedback. I could have told myself, "They just don't understand. They haven't been with me through this experience." But I knew they offered the wisdom and perspective I needed.

To be ready for the moments that require us to step out in courage, we have to walk with the wise. We don't need only people who are on our level and walking beside us; we need one or more people who are already up ahead of us who are willing to share the wisdom of what they have experienced and the mistakes they have made along the way. Find someone who is doing what you want to do; follow them, listen, and learn. The more you learn from these people, the more you become like them.

Maybe you have heard some of these sayings: "Well, if everyone jumped off a bridge, would you?" or "Walk with the wise—become wise!" But maybe you have never known whom and how to follow. You just liked whomever you liked and chose to spend time with those people. So let's talk about a step you can take that will help you walk with the wise.

Seek out leaders in your field and ask questions and take notes. The best way to grow is to surround yourself with those who are already steps ahead of you in the area or season you are in. The best teachers were once the best students. The best athletes, doctors, politicians, and world leaders were once learners and trainees. They understood that to be the best, they needed to learn from the best. Learn as much as you can. Ask a lot of questions. Take a lot of notes. Be open to being challenged. Find a mentor to meet with you, whether in person or virtually. It could be a parent, pastor, teacher, or leader. Mentorship will take you to the next level. Ask yourself these questions:

- Whom do I look up to?
- Am I teachable? Am I willing to grow? Can I truly allow someone to speak into my life and challenge me?
- Which voices speak into my life the most?

Environment Matters

Have you ever paused to take a look at your environment? What does that environment look like? Some of us are in unhealthy environments that distract us or detract from us. Some of us are in environments that don't do much of anything for us, neither making us better nor worse. Others of us are in environments that challenge us and inspire us to be all that God has called us to be. Your environment matters and has a bigger impact on who you are and who you are becoming than you might realize. Your environment can limit your growth or help launch you to your purpose.

When I think back to the good ole days when my dad coached me in basketball, he was a firm believer in this principle:

environment matters. Every summer tournament, he would set us up to play the hardest teams in the area. We were a 3A private school in Alabama playing 6A public schools in Georgia. Let me tell you, we were definitely the underdogs of every tournament. But that didn't intimidate or stop my dad. He liked putting us in environments that would challenge us and stretch us. During the season, my dad would have us scrimmaging against the boys' basketball team. Why did he do all this? He knew it would make us better. You don't grow by playing it safe. You grow, you improve, and you learn when you surround yourself with people who are better than you and when you seek out environments that challenge you.

You don't grow by playing it safe.

If we choose environments that limit us, we will never reach our full potential! We need environments that will challenge our thinking, that inspire our living, that push us to see the greatness within ourselves and help pull it out of us. Your environment matters.

Ask yourself these two questions and answer honestly:

- Do I feel challenged by my environment?
- Do I feel like I am consistently getting better, staying stagnant, or digressing backward?

If you want immediate results, go alone. If you want lasting results, go with others. We aren't made to do life alone; we are stronger and better together, but *who* the others are matters. Cultivate relationships with people who push you to be better. The right kind of people will always leave you wanting to be the best you can be.

Since your external surroundings influence your inner character, you would be wise to check your surroundings to see if they reflect who you want to be. To be ready for the tough moments of life, it is important to have the right people preparing you, pushing you, and praying for you. You have to be careful with what you allow into your life because it will influence everything: what you value, your decisions, how you view yourself, and how you see the world. **The people in your life will either push you toward your purpose or distract you from your purpose. The good news is you get to decide.**

Challenges on Your Surroundings

1. We aren't made to do life alone. Take a look at those around you and find the courage to remove the negative people from your life. Letting go of the relationships that aren't bettering you is an important step if you want to become more positive, fulfilled, and purposeful. Ask yourself, "Does my circle of friends . . ."

   - push me closer to God?
   - call out the greatness and potential inside me?
   - help me daily walk out my purpose?
   - stand with me in prayer and encouragement?
   - hold me accountable and keep me grounded?

2. Seek out environments where you can grow. Don't hold yourself back just to stay comfortable. If you're into sports, find a league that makes you a better player. If you are a writer, find a writers' group that will push your writing to be the best it can be. If you are passionate about helping people who are hurting, find an organization to volunteer with that stretches you in good ways.

3. Find a mentor, someone who is ahead of you and has already made a way for you. Someone who has been through what you are walking through and can challenge you and encourage you through it. Maybe it's a parent, a teacher, someone from your church, someone on social media, an author you admire, a pastor—think of someone you admire for their wisdom, and reach out to them. Mentorship will take you from good to great.

CHAPTER 11

PRESSURE'S ON

Staying True to Yourself in the High-Pressure Moments

Have you ever felt the weight of the world? Like all eyes are on you, just waiting for you to screw up? When you feel the pressure building, what do you do? There are two types of people in this world: people who fold under pressure and people who are propelled by pressure. Which are you?

I'm guessing most of you have heard the old adage "You are who you are when nobody is watching," suggesting, of course, that character is built, champions are made, and integrity is tested when nobody is around to judge or coach

> You are who you are when everyone is watching.

you. But I want to flip the script and offer a different approach: you are who you are when everyone is watching. Pressure's on. How will you respond?

All Eyes on You

Rivalry game. We're down by one with five seconds left, and I have the ball. The screen is set, and I go in and drive to the basket. The whistle blows. I was fouled. I look at the clock, and there is one second left. It all comes down to these free throws. I have to make both to secure the win. No pressure, right? I walk up to the line and take a few deep breaths. The whole gym is silent. *Swoosh.* I immediately look to my dad. He smiles and gives me a nice clap to affirm me. I hear his voice in my head: "Good job. One more." I am back on the line. Same routine. *Swoosh.* Immediately after the made basket, the buzzer goes off and there is screaming, hugging, and tears.

This is the kind of "all eyes on you" story we imagine in our heads, right? When the pressure hits, we make the game winner. We are the heroes in our own dreams. This is the kind of high-pressure moment I was comfortable with. This is the kind of high-pressure moment I wanted.

What I didn't expect was to be on national television on a reality TV show, with millions of people watching my love story for fun and entertainment every week. This wasn't what I imagined for myself. The pressure to make a free throw and win a game came with hundreds of people watching, not millions. I was used to the pressure that came with sports. I grew up with it. Television? I never imagined I would face that sort of pressure. This wasn't what I thought about when people said, "All eyes are on you. What are you going to do?"

As an athlete I was always prepped to be ready for those high-pressure moments. That is what we train for. Fourth quarter. Game on the line. Last play. Last shot. But how could I be ready for something like this? How would I know what to do when the whole world was watching me in a romantic relationship?

No matter what your "all eyes are on you" situation is or will be, one thing is for sure: **when the pressure hits, whatever is inside of you is what will come out of you.** Who you are when no eyes are on you is who you will be when all eyes are on you. The hours and days that were spent in practice with no one around will prepare you for the big games with everyone watching.

I Can Handle It

It had been nine weeks on *The Bachelor*, and I felt like I was slowly losing my mind. I was starting to be really homesick. Getting to see my family for only a few hours somehow made it even harder. Now that the hometown visits were over, it was time to head into the rose ceremony before fantasy suite week. Only three girls would move forward. On the dates the following week, Peter would have the option to invite each contestant to join him for a night in a fantasy suite. I had some big decisions to make.

When my name was called at the rose ceremony, I accepted the rose. Immediately after the ceremony, I asked if I could talk with Peter privately. I shared that fantasy suite week would be hard for me. I went on to share that I didn't think I would be able to move forward in the relationship if he were intimate with the other women. Fantasy suite week was known as an opportunity for couples to explore their physical relationship. I had only a few minutes to share my heart before we had to leave each other, and I walked away from the conversation feeling discouraged. I wasn't sure if he understood where I was coming from, and I didn't have enough time to dive into everything.

I couldn't sleep much that night. I wrestled with my thoughts. We boarded a plane and left for Australia early the next morning.

Throughout fantasy suite week, my thoughts and feelings tortured me. I got the last date of the week, which meant it would be two weeks since Peter and I'd had any quality time together. As he was on his other dates, I felt like I was going to hit my breaking point. I didn't know if I could continue with this process.

The day that I got to have my date with Peter finally arrived. After a long and hard week, the date was off to a surprisingly great start. During the day portion of the date, we climbed the tallest building in Gold Coast, Australia. They put harnesses on us and trained us how to climb the building safely. I had so much adrenaline, there was no room for fear. As we slowly made our way to the top of the building, what I felt physically directly paralleled what I felt internally. With each step came wind and opposition. Each step took me farther from the ground, the place of comfort and security. I felt the fight. I felt the loneliness that came with the journey. I felt the wind against me. I felt the opinions around me. I felt the pressures on top of me. I felt like one mistake and I'd slip; one wrong move could cost me everything. I felt the exhaustion and weariness. I knew getting to the top would be worth the struggle. I didn't know what "the top" meant for me, but I kept going.

The view from the top was breathtaking, overlooking the city, the beaches, the people. Every bit of uneasiness and worry vanished in that moment. On the top of that building, my problems and fears seemed so small. I was reminded that I am a part of something so much bigger than me. I felt a rush of peace as I saw all of Gold Coast, Australia. But that stillness and serenity came to a halting stop when the camera crew nudged us to make our way back down—that is, back down to face reality. Some hard conversations needed to be had, and I was not looking forward to having them.

When we arrived at dinner, I had a knot in my stomach.

This would be the conversation everyone had been waiting for. He grabbed my hand before we walked in and said to me, "You have nothing to worry about. Just trust me." Trust. Something that doesn't come easy for me, but I wanted to try. I knew there was a lot I needed to share with him. We were one week away from engagement, and this was a discussion we had to have.

As we sat, looking into each other's eyes with fear and hope, I could feel the tension and anxiety in the room. So much weight had been placed on this one conversation.

I took a deep breath, and before I knew it, words poured out of me. I told him, "When I was growing up, I made a commitment to myself. I decided I wanted to save myself for marriage. For me, I have always seen it as the day that I say 'I do' to the person that I want to spend the rest of my life with is the day that he is getting all of me—body, soul, and spirit, I'm his. I look at relationships and understand that both people may not have made the same life decisions, and I don't expect that. But this is the choice I have made for myself." I had just shared the most vulnerable thing I could share, and yet I could see the look of distress in his eyes. I knew what was coming—but I waited for him to tell me the words.

As I waited for what I knew was coming, I could hear my heart beating fast. It felt so loud, I was nervous the cameras would hear it! He began talking about how hard the week had been for him, and I sat there waiting for him to just tell me, but I could see in his eyes that he was afraid to tell me. My heart pounded faster and faster until he finally uttered the dreadful words, "I have been intimate with the other women." Even though I knew it was coming, hearing those words come out of his mouth felt like a dagger to my heart. He went on to share that this was his journey to find love and he did what he thought he needed to do. I told him, "This is my journey too. You may have done what you needed to do, but you might have lost me while doing it." He couldn't understand why I was so worried about what had happened in his other relationships and why that should affect ours. I looked at him bleakly and responded, "I just can't fathom on my engagement day, you get down on one knee and propose to me when six days before that you were intimate with someone else." The pressure of that moment was overwhelming.

I am going to take a shot in the dark here and say that your "pressure is on" moment probably didn't look anything like mine. Yours didn't consist of you dating a guy who was also dating twenty-nine other women while the whole world watched for fun, did it? I highly doubt it. But whatever your "pressure is on" moment looks like, the question always remains: How will you respond to the pressure? Most of the time in those moments of pressure, you will find yourself feeling alone in the unfamiliar. You will have to make tough decisions, sometimes without the help or advice of anyone around you. Lisa Bevere says, "Outward pressure is always an opportunity to be inwardly transformed."[1]

> We can stand firm in our convictions and stay true to ourselves, not because we are strong in moments of pressure but because we are strong in the moments of preparation.

As I have shared, I made a decision a long time ago to save myself for marriage. As we talked about in chapter 3, the promises we make to ourselves aren't always easy to keep in moments of pressure and temptation. However, we can stand firm in our convictions and stay true to ourselves, not because we are strong in moments of pressure but because we are strong in the moments of preparation.

I'm asked many questions about this choice. What caused you

to make that decision? Has it been hard to keep? Did you ever struggle or almost give in? Do guys think it is weird that you made that decision, or do they respect it?

I want to answer some of those questions as I share why I made that decision in the first place. As I grew up and my relationship with Jesus became a choice and not a passed-down expectation or religious requirement, I asked myself the tough questions, like who I wanted to be and how I wanted to handle certain situations. I knew I wanted to make some big decisions before I was faced with pressure or feelings. So I decided one day that I wanted to save myself for marriage. Nothing crazy happened. I didn't throw an "abstinence party" or make an announcement post on my Instagram. I was fifteen years old, and as I looked myself in the mirror, I decided that I wanted to save myself for the person God had for me.

I don't share my story to shame you, condemn you, or judge you if you haven't made the same life decisions as I have. My goal is not for you to feel like I am perfect and that I don't mess up— I'm not and I do. I've had moments where I have compromised my beliefs and convictions, moments that I have given into peer pressure, moments that I didn't take a stand for myself or for what I believe in, moments that I didn't step up to the line and knock down the free throw. We all make mistakes, we all fail, and we all have had times when we didn't respond well to pressure. My goal is to encourage you and challenge you that you *can* decide to stand up under pressure and withstand the temptations and obstacles. I want to be that friend who doesn't tell you only what you want to hear but what you need to hear. **You already have everything in you that you need to be all that you want to be. It's up to you to be it.** Life is hard and pressure will come, and if we don't make up our minds beforehand, there is a good chance we will fold.

Too many of us hope we will have the self-control in the heat of the moment to know when too far is too far—I'm not referring to just sex here. This can be regarding any societal or peer pressure to ignore your convictions, lower your standards, or conform to become someone you're not. I hate to break it to you, but you're not that strong. None of us are. That is why you have to prepare to stand firm before the option to fold ever arrives. That is why you have to prepare to win before the clock even starts. You have to prepare to say no before the temptation of yes comes wrapped in the form of a box of hot-and-ready donuts. You have to prepare for the high-pressure moments before they even arrive.

> Prepare for the high-pressure moments before they even arrive.

How will you be able to withstand the pressure? Pressure to be someone you aren't? Pressure to give in to temptation? Pressure to go against your convictions? Pressure to be easily misled or influenced? Because of how you prepare. Because of how you build. Those years of preparation get you ready for the moments of pressure so when they hit, you can rise up in confidence and say, "I can handle it."

How Do We Prepare Ourselves to Withstand High-Pressure Moments?

1. Know *why* you are preparing to stand firm in your values and convictions. Ask yourself, "Who do I want to be? What kind of life do I want to live? What do I value? How do I want to respond to certain situations?" Go back to those core values you wrote down from the earlier chapters!

2. Invest in yourself and build "muscle" to be able to withstand the pressure. Spend time in God's Word, prayer, and in community with those who will make you better.

3. Make decisions in advance. As you predecide what you want to do, tell your accountability partner so you have someone to hold you accountable. Don't trust yourself to make good decisions in the heat of the moment. As the saying goes, "When you fail to prepare, you prepare to fail." Don't set yourself up for failure.

4. As Matthew 5:37 (NKJV) reminds us, "Let your 'Yes' be 'Yes,' and your 'No,' 'No'." Say what you mean and mean what you say. When you make a decision, stick to it.

5. Put your conviction into action. Actions speak louder than words.

None of us are perfect, and unfortunately sometimes we fold under pressure. Instead of carrying around shame, acknowledge where you went wrong and learn from your mistakes. As Kelly Clarkson would say or, better yet, sing, "What doesn't kill you makes you stronger!" Keep going! I promise you, there will be plenty of moments to make up for any past mistakes.

Pressure Turned into Power

Diamonds are a girl's best friend, right?

I remember the first diamond I ever got. When I was thirteen, my dad bought me a diamond heart-shaped ring for Valentine's Day. Now, it wasn't a big diamond, but to me it was everything. I loved my ring and never took it off. I felt so powerful with it on, like nothing could get me down or stop me. When I had a bad day or someone did something that upset me, I would look down at that ring and be just fine. Why so? Because my daddy gave it to me, and I felt unstoppable. I felt on top of the world. One day I dropped my ring, and when I picked it up, I noticed that on the inside, engraved in small letters, was the word *strength*. I thought it quite an odd word to etch into a diamond ring to be handed out on Valentine's Day. Why not *love* or *joy* or my name or something? I asked my dad about it, and he responded, "Just like diamonds are made under pressure, strength is developed through resistance. And you are one strong girl. Don't ever forget it." My thirteen-year-old mind couldn't fully comprehend what my dad meant with all that, although I was moved by his belief in me. If my dad said so, it must be so. I am strong!

I have held on to those words and have seen them play out before my very eyes. The most beautiful things are created from pressure. The greatest leaders are built through opposition. The strongest athletes are built through resistance. Not many are willing to go through what it takes to get to where they desire to be. Orrin Woodward said, "Pressure squeezes effort out of winners and excuses out of losers."[2] Pressure is uncomfortable. Pressure hurts sometimes. But under pressure, what is within will come out. Always. Every time. Sometimes the most important thing is not what is happening around you but what is happening inside you.

> Not many are willing to go through what it takes to get to where they desire to be.

If there are two types of people—those who are made under pressure and those who are crushed under pressure—which are you? You get to choose. Pressure can build you or break you. Choose today to let pressure make you stronger.

Challenges on Pressure

1. Be intentional about what you consume because it affects who you are becoming and how you respond in moments of pressure. In these moments, there isn't another second to prepare or rehearse or practice one more time. What you've been prioritizing, the media you've been consuming, the people you've been letting influence you—all of that will unconsciously factor into your response. Because when pressure hits, what is inside of you will come out, so invest well!

2. Remember three things: who you are, what you value most, and your why. Under pressure, let it not be your emotions that guide your decisions but rather your convictions. Then, no matter what life throws at you, you will be prepared to stand firm and you will never lose yourself in moments of pressure.

3. Don't forget: diamonds are made under pressure. And you, my friend, are far more valuable than a diamond. Pressure will come, but instead of resenting and running from it, embrace it. Through preparation, you will develop the strength to face pressure with confidence.

CHAPTER 12

THE COST OF STANDING FIRM

Cultivating Faith and Strength through Moments of Loss

After my tough conversation with Peter, I walked away with hurt and doubt. I had already made clear to him that I didn't think I would be able to move forward if he was intimate with the other women. Even though he was, he still hoped I would understand and stay to see where our relationship would lead. I almost walked away that night and never looked back, but something in me told me to stay. I knew staying wouldn't mean that everything was okay and that we would go back to exactly how things were. If I were to stay, it would be because I didn't want to make an emotional decision in the heat of the moment. I wanted time to pray and have another conversation with Peter, one that wasn't full of shock and hurt on my end. So I decided to stay at least until the rose ceremony, though I didn't know if I would accept the rose or not.

Rose ceremony day arrived, and I was conflicted about what to do. Here I was, one week away from possible engagement. I should have been excited, full of love and hope, but I no longer felt safe or secure in the relationship. The more time I had to think, the more doubts filled my mind. I knew I needed to talk to Peter and hear his heart behind all that happened and also share my hurts and struggles. I didn't know if I could move forward, but I felt like I owed it to our relationship to have a conversation. I arrived at the rose ceremony, and when I did, the other two girls were already standing there. I wondered how long they had been there. The ceremony was on a mountaintop in Australia. It was beautiful—but with all the uneasy emotions welling up in my stomach, I couldn't enjoy the view. When Peter called my name and asked if I would accept the rose, I hesitated but finally nodded in acceptance. I had to leave almost immediately after and didn't get a chance to talk to him at the rose ceremony, but I had so much on my heart to share.

Two days later, we had our date. When I saw him, our relationship wasn't the same. What was once pure happiness and hope was now a wall of distrust. I didn't even have words to pair with the emotions I felt. As I tried to figure out how I could possibly move forward, the conversation continued to go in circles. I let him know I would no longer feel comfortable getting engaged with all that had happened, assuming that would be the deal breaker, yet he urged me to stay anyway, insisting he didn't need the engagement, just me. I wanted to stay because of my heart and feelings for him, but I felt trust had been broken, and I couldn't see how a relationship between us could go forward with our different perspectives on life and relationships. I thought I would have clarity by the end of the conversation, but I didn't. I left the conversation even more confused, yet we were three days away from engagement day, and I knew I had to make a decision. My head and my heart were at war with each other. I had already pre-decided what I was going to do. My head had made the decision, but the feelings in my heart made it difficult to follow through. After a lot of prayer and journaling, I knew what I needed to do. I just didn't want to do it.

The next day we had our last date. I couldn't even look Peter in the eyes. He was full of hope and excitement, and I dreaded what I knew was to come. I knew in that moment it was going to be harder than I thought. He could tell something was off, but he stayed hopeful. We flew around the Australian outback in a helicopter and spotted the well-known Uluru rock. Yet even with all the incredible and moving views, all I could think about was how hard it was going to be to walk away from him.

After the helicopter ride, we walked around for a bit. The outback was hot, and there were flies everywhere. Red dirt covered my white shoes, and my stomach twisted and turned as I dreaded the soon-to-be-had conversation. Peter pulled out a backpack with a picnic blanket and some sparkling cider. He poured a glass and made a toast. He started off toasting that our love was as strong as a rock—unshakable, unphased, immovable. "Great," I thought, "I have to break his heart after that?" I picked up my glass to toast, and I started off by reflecting on our journey and all that he taught me. I shared with him that he helped push me out of my comfort zone and challenged me to share not only my strengths but also my weaknesses and vulnerable feelings. He showed me that love can't be predicted or planned; it doesn't always look the same or come with a perfect formula or game plan.

Even though I felt so strongly for Peter, I knew deep down that there were major misalignments in our faith, morals, and lifestyles. I had to be willing to walk away from someone I loved, even though it was one of the hardest things I've ever done. As I shared with him these realizations, I saw the surprise and pain in his eyes. He argued back, attempting to convince me to stay and figure it out with him along the way. As tempting as that was, I knew I needed to leave.

As I got into the car and drove away, I felt so much loss in my heart. Someone that I loved and cared for was standing there crying and hoping I would turn around, yet I continued on. The pain of the loss was heavy; I felt crushed. I cared for Peter, and I sat in the car and cried for hours, thinking about all the amazing memories we created together.

After this day, over the course of several months, Peter and my journey continued with many confusing twists and turns and highs and lows. Yet the outcome still remained. Even with all the love in my heart, I knew deep down I couldn't give him what he was looking for and he couldn't give me what I needed. We weren't the best for each other, and we had to accept that and move on. Letting go of this relationship came with a cost, yet I trusted that this was the best decision for Peter and me and that my person was still out there and worth waiting for.

Reflecting on that journey, and many other seasons of my life, through the losses, heartbreaks, and failed relationships, I have learned a lot. I have learned to praise God for the losses because of what I gained in return. The losses turned into lessons, and the lessons turned into blessings. Many times I have planned out my life and what I want and expect it to look like. I try to control it and hold on to my plans as best I can, but the tighter I hold on to these dreams and expectations, the more I feel them slip away. Yet as I let go and trust God through the heartbreaks, losses, painful moments, and restless nights, I see

> The losses turn into lessons, and the lessons turn into blessings.

the blessings and what has been gained along the way. I see God orchestrating it all for my good.

We must be willing to let go of the lives we planned so we can have the lives that await us. As we become who we were created to be, we have to decide what we are willing to lose. Whether it's your status, your friends, your comfort, your control, your Instagram followers, your relationships, you name it, sometimes there is a cost to standing firm. Are you confident enough to let go?

The Exchange

Do you remember your first bike? I remember mine like it was yesterday: hot pink with sparkles, a white cushioned seat, with a cute white bell and tassels. It came with a matching pink, sparkly helmet. I remember waiting patiently for this bike. Every time we passed by it in Walmart, I would turn to my mom or dad and point with excitement: "This one! This is the one I want!" Weeks went by, and I didn't get my pink bike, but I kept holding on to hope! Christmas rolled around, and I bet you can guess what was sitting under my tree on Christmas morning. That's right, my pink bike!

I didn't even look at the rest of the gifts under the tree. This was the one thing I asked for and desperately had to have. Of course, it still had the training wheels on it. I have heard the stories of most kids being afraid of hopping on their bikes and venturing off on their own. Not me. I got on that bike, and my parents had to chase me down to keep me from venturing too far.

My friends would come over every day and bring their bikes. We would often vote on who had the best bike—mine would always win. I was so proud of my bike and loved to show it off. It was the best gift I had ever received. Months and months passed by, and I still came home after school and ran to hop straight on that bike.

One day my dad came home from work and asked if I would give my bike to my younger sister Mallory. I was taken aback that he would make such a request. This was the best gift he had ever given me! But I couldn't say no to my dad. I looked up at him and said, "Daddy, anything but my bike. She can have my new American Girl doll or my new toys for the dollhouse." But he insisted that she needed the bike. At first I walked away upset and frustrated. How could my dad ask me to give up something so precious to me? After taking the night to think about it, I woke up the next day, and I called my dad into my room. When he came in, I handed him my pink helmet, and with tears in my eyes, I replied, "She needs it more than me, so she can have it, Daddy."

My dad smiled big and told me to follow him. When I followed him out of my room, he walked outside and led me to the most beautiful bike I had ever seen. It was bigger, shinier, and without training wheels! I wondered how my dad could afford this bike, but the thought was pushed aside when I saw the pack of stickers that came with the bike that I could use to decorate the bike and my helmet.

I rushed up to my dad and hugged him tight. "What did I do to deserve this?" I asked. I'll never forget his response. He told me, "Because you gave up good for best." He went on to teach me a lesson about how often when we go after our dreams and when we pursue God, it might come with a cost and an exchange that we might not always understand at the time, but when we lay down "good," we give God the opportunity to give us "best." I am sure he threw in some basketball analogies or quotes too; I will never forget that moment with my dad. Even though I didn't understand why my dad, who loves me so much, would ask me to give up something I loved, I trusted him. It turned out that what I gave up was small compared to what I gained!

There have been many moments when I've wanted to cling to what I have, even if I know it isn't God's best for me. Are you holding on so tightly to harmful or unnecessary relationships, habits, or activities that it seems impossible to let go?

Sometimes the very things God asks us to lay down he returns back to us tenfold. When we are forced to let go of something we really long for—whether it's taken away, or it seems it will never be given—it's crushing, disappointing, and frustrating. Many times it requires us to surrender what we hold close to our hearts. But friend, be encouraged: God will return to you what you were willing to lay down, not only meeting your expectations but surpassing them.

> God will not only meet your expectations but surpass them.

So what is your exchange? Maybe you laid down something and got something even better in return, or maybe you didn't lay it down but felt it was taken from you. It is important to know that what is meant for you will be yours. What may feel like a loss right now you will later see as a big gain!

Consider the Cost

Let me tell you guys about the time I won $8,000 on *The Price Is Right*. That's right. *The Bachelor* wasn't my first TV debut. In 2018 I went on *The Price Is Right* and walked away with some cha-ching! It is a crazy story. There was a group of us in Los Angeles serving at The Dream Center. We decided that before we headed back home to Alabama, we wanted to do something fun. We found some available tickets for *The Price Is Right*, and we reserved them. It said in big, bold letters on the front of the tickets, "DON'T BE LATE."

The day finally arrived for us to head to the studio for *The Price Is Right* taping. We were so excited and made sure to wake up extra early since we couldn't be late! We called our Uber and headed to the studio. It gave us an estimate of twenty minutes until we arrived. About ten minutes into the drive, we noticed the time kept climbing up because the traffic was so bad. We were a little nervous but hoped it would clear out. Boy, were we wrong. We underestimated LA traffic. What should have been a twenty-minute drive turned into an hour drive. By this point we were panicking, yelling, and directing our driver to cut people off, run red lights, and "get us there faster!" Poor guy, he thought he would have just another normal day of driving tourists around LA—not with us he didn't! I am surprised he didn't get pulled over.

We pulled up to the studio right on the dot, 10:00 a.m.! But when we got out, we noticed there was a line of people. We tried to get the attention of the people who worked there to let them know we had tickets, but we couldn't. Minutes passed by and the clock was ticking. Finally, an employee walked over, and we showed him our tickets; we were ready to go in and win some money! He looked at us like we were crazy and replied, "It's 10:02. You're too late." We tried explaining our situation and that we had been waiting in line, but he wasn't in the mood for our excuses. The guy told us we would have to come back another day. We insisted that we couldn't come back because we were from out of town. He finally negotiated with us that if we could come back for the next show-time that same day and not be late, he could most likely get us in.

When we came back the second time, we showed up at the

studio close to an hour early. The guy laughed, impressed with our ability to show up not just on time but early, and he got us in. We went through the whole process, which involved a couple of interviews as they selected their first four contestants. And as we waited, we pulled up old *Price Is Right* episodes because I had never seen one before. The group with me thought it was crazy that we were about to be on a show I had never seen before. They started trying to explain how it works and the different games there might be. I was excited—it sounded fun!

When we finally got inside the studio, it looked a lot smaller than what I saw on the videos. We sat down in our assigned seats and cheered as the camera swung over the crowd. When Drew Carey, the host, came out, he welcomed everyone in the crowd and went on to call out the first four names to begin the show. James . . . Bianca . . . Liam . . . Madison Prewett! I realized, "Wait, that's me! Oh no, I don't know what I'm doing—here goes nothing!" I walked up to my podium jumping and clapping. The first round of bidding happened, and . . . my mind went blank. I don't even remember what number I guessed. I thought, "Well, that didn't go well. I've got to get my head in this!"

The opportunity came to guess again. Before I knew it, I yelled out, "$850!" Immediately, Drew Carey looked down at the card with the correct price and yelled, "$899! Madison, come on up!" I couldn't believe I guessed it right. I had no idea what was happening. I went on stage and played the game called "Put It in the Bag." The goal was to line up each grocery item with the correct price. There were items ranging from chicken wings to vitamins, and I had to guess the price of each item. As Drew approached each grocery bag with a price on it, the crowd would go crazy, screaming, "Chicken wings!" There was one instant I couldn't hear clearly because everyone seemed to be yelling something different.

To confirm, I flapped my arms up and down like wings to signify the wings, and I watched for the heads of the crowd to nod up and down to ensure I was selecting the right grocery item.

Near the end, I became more nervous. For the next level, more money was on the line. I ended up stopping a little short, and I won $8,000 cash! That story is still so crazy to me. If our day had gone according to our original plan, I most likely wouldn't have gotten called up to play and walked away with eight grand. When we weren't allowed in earlier that day, we were upset and frustrated that our plans were messed up and our expectations weren't met, but something happened that was even greater than what we expected. What seemed like a loss in the moment turned out to be a big gain!

Now, nearly missing my "big break" on a game show is a pretty low-stakes scenario. But something about that experience called to mind the kind of life that Jesus calls us to. Hang with me for a minute. When we sign on to follow him, we are never told that we won't suffer or experience loss. In fact, many Christians through-out history have spoken of the cost of following Jesus. I don't know your situation and the losses you have experienced. I am sure some of you have walked through tragic loss, and I am so sorry for the pain and suffering that has come with it. I wish I could tell you that life will get easier and better and you won't ever experience another loss, but unfortunately, life is full of loss. Because the world is a broken and sinful place, we lose things and people we love. We suffer for what we believe. We experience heartache.

In the midst of that pain, it's tempting to wonder why we should stick with Jesus if we are still vulnerable to the sting of loss. Why keep showing up to church or spending time in Scripture or staying committed to purity when some days faith feels more like a chance game of "Put It in the Bag," hoping we win some kind of blessing? When the losses pile up and our hearts are worn out, we feel the weight of what it means to be a disciple. But sometimes what seems like a loss really does turn out to be our gain.

In the book of Philippians, Paul takes this idea even further, saying that anything he has gained he counts as loss because it all pales in comparison to knowing Jesus and having the hope of eternity with him (Philippians 3:7–11). This idea might cause you to scratch your head; it definitely makes me do a double take. Following Jesus not only means I will lose or have to give up certain things, it also means what he gives us—salvation, forgiveness of sins, his presence, and the gift of eternal life—is so much more than anything I would mark as a gain.

Philippians 3:7–11 says:

> But whatever were gains to me I now consider loss for the sake of Christ. What is more, I consider everything a loss because of the surpassing worth of knowing Christ Jesus my Lord, for whose sake I have lost all things. I consider them garbage, that I may gain Christ and be found in him, not having a righteousness of my own that comes from the law, but that which is through faith in Christ—the righteousness that comes from God on the basis of faith. I want to know Christ—yes, to know the power of his resurrection and participation in his sufferings, becoming like him in his death, and so, somehow, attaining to the resurrection from the dead.

This puts the *Price Is Right* moment in perspective for me. I nearly lost the opportunity to gain something greater because we misjudged the traffic. What else should I count as loss so that I might gain knowing Jesus and the blessings he gives those who love him? **Following him might cost you everything you thought you wanted, but what you gain is everything you really needed.**

Breaking up with someone you know isn't God's best for you feels like a loss; the thought of losing that person seems too painful to bear. Yet later in life, as you walk down the aisle on your wedding day, you will be eternally grateful you had the courage to make that decision. It might be hard to let go of the friend you have been close to for so long, the one who knows everything about you. It might be scary to quit your job, but trust and believe deep down that what awaits you has far greater worth.

I have learned that sometimes blessings come in the form of tears, bad breaks, and reroutes. Yes, these may seem like strangely wrapped gifts. But let's not miss our blessings just because we don't love the packaging.

Challenges on Standing Firm

1. Be ready to sacrifice your plans and desires in order to follow where God is leading you. Often, when your made-for-this-moment opportunity arrives, it will come with a cost. When you respond to moments of pressure with courage, your losses will turn into lessons, and those lessons will become blessings.

2. Trust that God's plan for you is greater than you could ever imagine. Sometimes a loss might cost you everything you thought you wanted, but what you gain is everything you really needed. We often have expectations of what we think is best for us, but our best is dull in comparison to God's best. That is why we have to trust. Isaiah 55:8–9 says, "'My thoughts are not your thoughts, neither are your ways my ways,' declares the LORD. 'As the heavens are higher than the earth, so are my ways higher than your ways and my thoughts than your thoughts.'"

3. Don't judge a book by its cover. We have heard that phrase a million times. It still reigns true. Often the book ends up being much different from our initial judgment based on the cover. Sometimes our answers to prayer, too, come wrapped in boxes that look much different than what we ordered. Don't judge a blessing by its packaging!

CHAPTER 13

THE FIGHT FOR YOUR MOMENT

Standing Firm with Strength, Grace, and Courage

Let me tell you a little about my dad and our relationship on the court. My dad is a tough guy. He would say he doesn't "put up with any crap." He requires people to give 110 percent—nothing less—and he always expects his players to go the extra mile. And his expectations of his other players dulled in comparison to those he had for me. He constantly stayed on me, and if anyone—and I mean anyone—on the team was slacking, didn't know a play, or didn't have their head in the game, it was my fault. I was also the point guard, so he would constantly remind me that, as the PG, my role was to be the leader, which meant when I was doing well, the team was doing well; when I was off, the team was off. This was something I had grown to accept.

My dad and I fought a lot throughout the time I played for him. I would often come home and tell my mom I didn't want to play anymore because Dad was so tough on me. Dealing with the weight of my dad's pressure on me was hard sometimes. Other times, it was awkward, like when we would have to get in the car, ride home, and have dinner together after having a fight on the court.

One fight in particular sticks out. We were playing in a tournament. We had already played one game that day, and we were in the fourth quarter of our last game. As I was going after a loose ball, I was elbowed in the face and then shoved into the scorer's table. I was pretty sure I broke my nose. My dad yelled, "What is taking so long? Get up and get back in the game!" I walked over with a bloody nose and said, "Dad, I think I broke it!" His response was, "Well, I guess we will have to get that checked after the game. Get back in!"

I would have loved nothing more than to watch the clock run out from the sidelines and go home and lie down. But you know what kept me in the game until the end of the fourth quarter? *My dad's voice on the sidelines.* As harsh as his words felt at times, I knew that ultimately he pushed me to be better, to lead the team, and to fight until the final buzzer rang out because he loved me and knew I had more to give, bloody nose and all. When I heard my dad's voice, I could narrow my focus and drown out the other sounds in the gym. I could give a little more. I could fight until the last moment.

Thinking over my life so far, I've felt that fourth-quarter exhaustion more than I would have liked. You probably have too. Many times the sidelines look more comfortable. Some days losing seems like a guarantee, so why even try? Sometimes we ask God, "Why does it feel like I am the one getting punished even though

I didn't do anything wrong?" Friends, these are the moments for which we have been preparing. And who you listen to in those moments can make or break you.

We are approaching that fourth-quarter moment, and I want each and every one of you to be able to fight through it with strength, grace, and courage. As Sadie Robertson likes to say, "Anybody can quit. Only a real champion and a person of character and strength can keep going and refuse to give up."[1] When the struggle for your identity feels like too much, when staying committed to your decisions about the kind of woman you want to be feels impossible and exhausting, when you're down with a bloody nose and want to head to the bench—what voices are speaking to you from the sidelines? Who are you listening to when it counts the most? Who is keeping you in the game?

Who Are You Listening To?

There is so much negativity in the world today. Spend three minutes on social media and you'll be exposed to a dangerously high dosage of hate, judgment, and reactionary outrage. Amid all this noise, it is imperative to listen to the right voices, the voices that encourage you and challenge you to be your best. You can't control what others say, but you can control which words you believe and which ones you reject. The voices of negativity, condemnation, and hate are often some of the loudest voices, yet if we learn to tune them out, we can be at peace.

> You can control which words you believe and which ones you reject.

I could never have anticipated the judgmental, critical, hateful words that were directed at me after my experience on *The Bachelor*.

189

I knew people may not agree with my stand for faith or my choices, but I had no idea people who did not know me could be so cruel. You would be floored by some of the repulsive comments I received through direct messages on social media. By people who do not know me. By people who felt they had a right to say offensive things to me and about me because of what they saw on a show. Things they could say behind a computer screen and under a fake account. Things that made them laugh and feel powerful with an intention to hurt me. Things that were meant to tear me down, cause me pain, and destroy me. They didn't know me. They didn't consider the degree of damage that could be done by their words. They just lashed out, without consideration, without a second thought.

After the show ended, these comments and critiques had a profound effect on my mind and body. I had so much anxiety. It affected my appetite, my sleep, and my mood. I lost so much weight, and my skin and hormones were affected in ways I had never experienced. I want to share some of the negative comments that were sent to me after the show:

- "Just want to say f——— your family and your weird a——religion and values."
- "Madi has spider lashes. Please someone teach this girl how to do her mascara!"
- "You make me cringe. (Barf emojis)"
- "You only went on the show to be an influencer. You only care about yourself and want to be famous."
- "You are fake. And a liar."
- "I hope you die, you stupid virgin."

One of these statements alone was enough to send me into a funk, if I'm honest. Countless messages like these crowded my

DMs and comments. The other girls from the show shared my pain, as their DMs were also full of vulgar and unspeakable messages that made them cry all night.

Words have lasting impact. They don't just go away. They stay attached to us for years. People have ended relationships over words, lost jobs over words, battled depression and poor self-image over words, and even ended their lives over words. You've heard the phrase "Sticks and stones may break my bones, but words will never hurt me." Not true. Bones heal, but a spirit that has been broken by hurtful words can affect a person for years, or even a lifetime. Poisonous words can lead to sickness or even death.

Every person you come in contact with is going through something. It may not be obvious on the outside, but everyone is facing some type of battle. Many times I would post a picture of me smiling, and everyone would assume that the picture signified that I was happy and confident. But on the inside I was struggling with the new world I had been thrown into and the harsh and hurtful words of others that seemed to stay glued to my memory. Everyone is facing a battle, whether you can see it or not.

I want to challenge you to be the person who offers a word of encouragement. Words often impact people for decades, providing either the courage to press on or one more reason to give up. Be the one who speaks life into someone's situation. A simple word of hope could change the direction of someone's life.

One day as I was praying to God, frustrated that this was my new life and hurt by the careless words of others that weighed so heavy on my soul, I found a note in my journal that I used during my time on the show: "I can't control what other people say, but I can control what I listen to and what I allow to affect me." Hurting people often want to hurt others so they aren't alone in their pain. Jealous people tend to try to discredit or harm the reputation of the person they are jealous of. Mean people like to bring other people down.

Reading through my journal, I felt challenged by the very words I had written a few months before. I realized if I sat around letting the words of people who don't know me or even care about me stop me from fulfilling my purpose, then they would win. And I refused to let them win. So the more people who sent hate, the more it spurred me on to make a difference. The more they took shots at me, the more I poured into my purpose. Haters will hate, but only I can decide if I will let them hold me back.

I had to realize that for every hundred positive comments, there was one negative. Isn't it funny how the one negative seems to somehow carry more weight than the many positives? I decided I had to focus on the comments that built me up, encouraged me, and spoke truth. I refused to let the negative comments enter my heart. I stayed away from message boards and social media sites or accounts that promoted gossip and hate. You have no idea how much this protected me from reading words that had potential to hurt me or discourage me. People can be cruel, but if you refuse to listen to them or allow them access to your mind or heart, they cannot bring you down.

Surround yourself with people who cheer you on. People who speak life to you. People who use words to build you up. Listen to those people. Ignore the ones who don't. Let me share a few of the positive comments I received after the show:

- "I have never been a religious person, but I decided to give my life to Christ after watching you on the show."
- "I decided to wait until marriage since you showed me it's not weird or something to be ashamed of. I feel like now I can be brave in my convictions."

- "After last night's episode where Madi talked about her standards and the choices she's made for herself, my ex-boyfriend texted me and apologized for not honoring me and treating me with respect."
- "Madi, you were the light this world needed. I have a four-month-old daughter, and I pray that I can teach her values as strong and deep as yours. You handled everything you went through with faith, kindness, upmost respect, and smiles."
- "I wish I could go back in time and be just like you. I'm ten years older, but I look up to you so much."
- "Thank you for being such a positive role model for young girls around the world! You stood up for what you believe in, in the midst of a world that is constantly telling you not to! You inspired me to walk closer to the Lord every day, and I thank you for that!"
- "Your eyelashes are amazing! Please tell me what mascara you use."

These were the words I needed to focus on!

Friend, who are you listening to? There will always be people who don't agree with you or like you or who can't be happy for your successes. But as hard as it is, you must block out the negative voices that try to tear you down and keep you from fulfilling your purpose. If you aren't careful, you can let one negative word create an avalanche of feeling like everyone feels this way about you and that no one likes you. That is a lie! Don't go there in your mind. What a person says to you or about you does not define you. They can't decide who you are. They can't play a single role in your identity if you

> What a person says to you or about you does not define you.

193

don't let them. Their words are just words. Only by tuning them out can we move forward in our purpose.

Find your circle of friends that cheer you on. Listen to them. Tune out all the others. I love this quote by John Maxwell: "Small people will tear you down, but big people will make you feel bigger than you thought you could be."[2] Your life is too short and too valuable to sit around worrying about what negative people are saying about you. Know who you are, and listen to the right voices. The voices that say you matter. The voices that say you are enough. The voices that say you have value.

Pastor Craig Groeschel said, "You are not who others say you are. You are who God says you are."[3] If someone told you that you are not good enough, do not believe them. If someone says that you are not loved, do not believe them. If someone tells you that you are a mistake, do not believe them. You are more than enough, you are deeply loved, and you were created on purpose for a purpose. When you listen to God's voice and what he says about you, then you will begin finding strength in your own voice. It's relatively easy to block internet trolls, but it's really difficult to block the negative voice in your own head that tears you down. When you surround yourself with God's truth and other people who lift you up, you're better equipped to silence your inner voice, which attempts to tear you down, and become an uplifting voice in your own life.

Some of you might be scared to step out into what you are called to do because you have believed words that aren't true. I've found that the best way to stop believing those lies is to replace them with truth. I turn to the Bible to hear truth from the voice that will never lead me astray. Psalm 139:14 says, "I praise you because I am fearfully and wonderfully made." Jeremiah 1:5 says, "Before I formed you in the womb I knew you, before you were born I set you apart."

Listening to the right voices is essential for walking in your purpose and making every moment count. I'm reminded of Esther once again. She was faced with a huge decision: does she confront the king and risk death? Or does she stay silent and watch the destruction of her people? Esther was a person just like us: she probably wanted to play it safe, not speak up, stay in her comfort zone, not make waves. In light of her inner turmoil and indecision, her cousin Mordecai spoke up and challenged her to be who she was created to be: "If you keep quiet at a time like this, deliverance and relief for the Jews will arise from some other place, but you and your relatives will die. Who knows if perhaps you were made queen for just such a time as this?" (Esther 4:14 NLT). Esther paid attention to who was talking to her, took heart, and responded with courage. She chose to speak up and make her moment count, and God honored that.

She entered a high-stakes scenario brave enough to lose, strong enough to stand. And in that same way, we can choose who we listen to when the pressure is on. By surrounding ourselves with the voices that uplift us and challenge us to be all we were created to be, we will find the strength, grace, and courage to discover all that God has in store for us.

> Be brave enough to lose, strong enough to stand.

Strength, Grace, and Courage

As I look back at the last season of my life, I see three words rise to the surface: *strength*, *grace*, and *courage*. These three words mark the kind of woman I want to be, and I believe that everything up to this point in my life has been pointing me toward them.

Not only are they shaping me, but I think *strength*, *grace*, and *courage* are words that can also define our generation. I want to be surrounded by other young women who are strong, brave, and graceful, women who respond to the pressures of the world from a place of unshakable confidence in who they are. My time on *The Bachelor* helped me grow, and I became stronger in standing firm and standing up for what I believe in. My preparation in knowing and living by my values gave me the strength I needed when I faced temptation.

Although I felt a lot of pressure knowing millions of people were watching me, I knew that other women would find their own strength in my decision to stand firm in my convictions. Maybe today you don't feel brave or strong. Maybe you feel clumsy and like you've made a mess of your life so far. But look to your right and to your left. There is someone who wants to encourage you and see you thrive. Sometimes we have to borrow one another's strength so that we can find our own.

No, we don't respond to all of life's difficult moments flawlessly and gracefully or with great courage. When we expect perfection from ourselves, moments of pressure will become exponentially more anxiety-inducing. God has endless grace that he is constantly unfolding in our lives. When we focus on his grace rather than our imperfections, we are able to see his hand at work in our lives and feel his strength in the midst of our weaknesses.

As you now know, I've made a lot of mistakes. I'm not a perfect Christian, daughter, friend, or role model. And that's not what I'm trying to be. I'm not preparing so that I can be perfect; I'm preparing for all life throws at me so that I can be proud of who I am and what I've accomplished. God's purpose for your life does not require perfection, but it does require preparation. Progress, not perfection, always.

In moments of pressure, though, calling to mind these truths is so, *so* difficult. The night of the finale was the biggest test of my preparation so far. I was blindsided, hurt, and confused. I didn't know where God was in that moment, for I felt so alone and hurt. But as I reflect on that time now, I know he was there with me. His voice and the voice of my mom were reminding me to be strong and courageous. I know he prepared me for that moment throughout my life.

In the end, I came out on the other side with confidence in who I am and who I am becoming. Even though it didn't feel like it at the time, strength, grace, and courage were buried deep in my heart. Though feeble at the time, those roots kept me grounded and composed. I didn't run or hide or never show my face again, because I knew who I was, and I had to trust that I would be okay if I held on to that truth. Now I look ahead to my future and know there is more for me.

And I want to be ready for whatever "more" looks like. Being made for these moments isn't a one-time deal. This is a lifelong work. To stay firmly planted in Christ. To cultivate community that surrounds me with support. To love others well. To face my past with bravery.

In the Message translation of 2 Corinthians 4:16–18, I love the way Paul's powerful words ring out the hope that is found in Jesus: "So we're not giving up. How could we! Even though on the outside it often looks like things are falling apart on us, on the inside, where God is making new life, not a day goes by without his unfolding grace. These hard times are small potatoes compared to the coming good times, the lavish celebration prepared for us. There's far more here than meets the eye. The things we see now are here today, gone tomorrow. But the things we can't see now will last forever."

Small potatoes compared with a feast—I love that thought! Even though we may be struggling, God is creating new life in us and preparing us for a future and purpose that is even greater than our wildest dreams.

Whether you are in a season of preparation or a moment of pressure, I want to challenge you to trust that God is using this time in your life to create something new in you. It is time to rise up and embrace every moment with courage and confidence. God has so much more in store for you.

Whether your moment of courage requires speaking up, staying silent, taking a stand, fighting for justice on behalf of someone else, or amplifying the voices of those around you, there will always be a choice. Fight or flight will kick in; your heart will skip a beat as the adrenaline flows through your body. Amid all the noise around you, choose to keep going, and listen to that still, small voice encouraging you to fight for your moment with strength, grace, and courage. **You're not finished making moments!**

ACKNOWLEDGMENTS

As I said earlier, if you want immediate results, go alone. If you want lasting results, go together. I have learned it's not always about how fast I can get there; it's about going further than I thought I could go and leaving a greater impact than I even thought possible. I couldn't have done this book on my own. I am grateful for all of you who helped make this book possible.

To my parents, Chad and Tonya: Thank you for believing in me, supporting me, and never giving up on me, even when I was stubborn and difficult. Thank you for raising me in the church. Thank you for teaching me and showing me the significance of following Christ. Thank you for being firm in your faith and convictions. Thank you for the many sacrifices you have made to love and lead our family well. Mom, you embody true love and grace, and you are a mother to many. Dad, you embody true courage and discipline. You have shown me the importance of preparation and practice. You two have had the greatest impact on who I am today. You both were the first examples to me of true moment-makers.

My sisters, Mallory and Mary Mykal: I have never loved anyone more. I would do anything for you two. Thank you for standing by my side through all my hardest seasons. I hope you know I will always be a safe place for you when you are down. I will always champion you. I will always challenge you to be the best you can be. I see two world-changers when I look at you both. I love you more than words could ever say.

My grandmothers, Glenda and Delores: Thank you for being my biggest cheerleaders and prayer warriors! I wouldn't be where I am without your prayers and support. I thank God that I have both of you to lean on. You both are examples of women who have had to overcome a lot of adversity and setbacks yet didn't give up. You have shown me the power of the "next play." God isn't done using you both. I am better because of you. Thank you for your wisdom and love. They mean the world to me.

My great-grandmother, Juliette: I owe much of my stubbornness and fighter spirit to you. Although sometimes it may be difficult to understand or hard to steward, I rejoice in it. You are undeniably you, and you are unshakable in what you believe. Thank you for showing me what it looks like to stand firm in conviction.

My best friend, Erica: Thank you for standing by my side through the highs and lows and being my person through thick and thin. Your friendship is an answered prayer and breath of fresh air. You inspire me with how you love Jesus, and every moment I spend with you leaves me encouraged and challenged. I have watched you over the years and have seen many come to Jesus because of your joyous spirit and burdened heart for the hurting. Keep shining bright and making it matter.

Brandon and Amy Isbell: I have learned so much through your leadership and intentionality. I know wherever life takes me, you two will always have a big role in my life. Thank you for the hours of prayer (and many other sacrifices that were made) that have shaped me into who I am today. I cherish you both.

LoriAnn and Keith Biggers: I feel a part of the Biggers family, and I wouldn't want it any other way. Thank you for loving me and for opening up your home and hearts to me. The moment I met you, LoriAnn, I knew you were special and that we would have a strong relationship. Thank you for taking me in as one of your own. I love you both so much.

Pastor Scotty Howard: Your prayer life is inspiring. Your convictions are unwavering. Your calling is undeniable. You are one of the biggest contributors to where I am today. Thank you for the friend you are to our family and the many prayers you have sowed—the harvest is coming! May God bless your family richly.

Deann Hadaway: You have been a shoulder to cry on, a hug of joy and excitement, and a charge-hell-with-a-water-gun type of mentor. Thank you for being someone I can always count on. Your life, your marriage, and your heart inspire me.

Jeanine, my roommate, champion, friend, and sister: You have been one of the biggest answered prayers. I know with all my heart that we were put into each other's lives for such a time as this. Thank you for being a consistent and dependable friend. You have walked me through many highs and many lows. I believe this is just the beginning for you and me. The best is yet to come! You are stronger than you think you are. I will always be your biggest cheerleader.

Pastor Don and Sara Davis: Thank you for being uncompromising in your faith and convictions. You two helped play a major role in laying a solid foundation for me from a young age. My first personal encounter with the Holy Spirit happened at camp AFA, and I will forever remember that moment. I cherish the words and prayers you both have prayed over my family and me. And I praise God every day for your influence and leadership that you have had on my parents, who are God's greatest gift to me. Thank you for being the leaders and pastors that you are. Love you both always.

Gracen Jade: Since I first laid eyes on you, I knew you were special. You have an undeniable and contagious joy about you while also possessing a rare strength and boldness. When you are around, people can't help but smile. When I have a bad day, I just think about your laugh or pull up a picture of that perfect smile. Even though your story might not look like everyone else's, you are more loved than you could ever imagine. I believe with everything in me that you are destined for greatness and your potential is limitless. You will help so many who have broken pasts and hard stories. Through your joy and strength they will come to see themselves the way they were always meant to. I couldn't possibly love you more. I will forever be your biggest cheerleader.

Bruce and Brandy Pearl: I am beyond grateful for your love and support. You both make everyone around you want to be better. You are coaches not only on the court but off the court as well. You challenge, cheer on, and empower those around you to be better and go further than they even thought possible. You make champions not just out of teams but out of people too. You have a special calling on your life, and you have touched many people. I am so grateful I got to be one of them. Love always and family forever.

Maddie McClendon: I dedicate so much of this message to you—a queen, an Esther, a moment-maker. You have shown me true strength, grace, and courage. When life threw its hardest punches, you walked with grace and joy. When the pressures and struggles around you seemed overwhelming and unknown, you kept walking in strength. Even as you took your last breaths on this earth, you did it with courage—unafraid and prepared. You have shown me the importance of living life with urgency and purpose. I pray that through your story and journey, many people will be helped, saved, and healed. Maddie strong, forever.

My Fedd Agency team: Esther, Danielle, Allison, and Tori, you are hardworking and brilliant go-getters. Thank you for never letting me settle for good enough and always pushing me to be the best I can be. I can do what God has called me to do because of you. Esther, thank you for the vision you had for this book and stepping in the trenches with me to carry it out. You guys are a true dream team. I love you all.

My Zondervan team: Stephanie, Carolyn, and everyone else who has contributed to editing and publishing this book, thank you for believing in me, for taking a chance with me, and for taking me as I am but helping me become all God has called me to be. I can't believe I get to work with you guys. Every day, I wake up and thank God for the blessing of having you all beside me. Because of you guys, a dream I had as a little girl came to life! Thank you for pouring your time, energy, and hearts into this message. Because of you, I believe, people all around the world will be impacted.

Lysa TerKeurst and her family: Your passion, creativity, and heart for Jesus are evident in all you do. You inspire me with the strength and grace you carry. Thank you, Lysa, and your team for caring about this message and offering wisdom and insight on how to make it the best it can be. You are someone I look up to, and I cherish our relationship. You have also raised amazing daughters, whom I love very much! I believe in you and love you.

Lori Krebs: You have seen it all and stood by my side through some of my roughest and hardest moments. You challenge me and push me to do more and be more. Thank you. Thank you for being someone I can trust and someone I can count on.

ABC and Bachelor Nation: Thank you for your grace, patience, and support. We have been through a lot together, and I am stronger because of it.

To all my other friends and family: I wish I could name every single one of you. Thank you for having my back, encouraging my spirit, and holding me accountable. You are my iron sharpening iron. I thank God for all of you every day.

To the women who have paved the way, the true pioneers of faith: we thank you. This message wouldn't be made possible without your sacrifices, boldness, and conviction. I hope to be as bold and courageous as you were.

To you, my reader friend: I wish I could give you a big hug and look you in the eyes. I have spent months, weeks, days, and hours praying for you and thinking about you. I hope you know how loved you are. I hope you feel empowered to walk in strength, conviction, and courage, knowing your value and purpose. No matter what your journey may look like, you too were made for this moment. I believe in you and send you my love.

NOTES

Chapter 1: Courage for Your Moment

1. Bethany Hamilton in Laura Lynn, "The Courage That's Bravery," Teen Beat, *Hood County News* (Granbury, TX), August 21, 2004, 3B.

Chapter 2: Ready or Not

1. Christine Caine (@ChristineCaine), "Jesus walks on the very waves we think will drown us," Twitter, February 3, 2021, 12:19 p.m., https://twitter.com/christinecaine/status/1357015758967029762.

Chapter 3: The Power of the Preseason

1. James A. Baker and Steve Fiffer, *"Work Hard, Study . . . And Keep Out of Politics!"* (Evanston, IL: Northwestern University Press, 2006), 5.

Chapter 4: Say Goodbye to the Snooze Button

1. Chris Hodges, *The Daniel Dilemma: How to Stand Firm and Love Well in a Culture of Compromise* (Nashville: Thomas Nelson, 2017), 126.
2. Gretchen Rubin, "What You Do Every Day Matters More Than What You Do Once in a While," *Gretchen Rubin* (blog), November 7, 2011, https://gretchenrubin.com/2011/11/what-you-do-every-day -matters-more-than-what-you-do-once-in-a-while/.

Chapter 5: Deal with It

1. Perry Noble, *Unleash! Breaking Free from Normalcy* (Carol Stream, IL: Tyndale, 2012), 33.

Chapter 6: The Price of Unforgiveness

1. *Living in Freedom Every Day,* (Birmingham, AL: 2004), 82.
2. Lysa TerKeurst, *Forgiving What You Can't Forget* (Nashville: Thomas Nelson, 2020), 200.
3. TerKeurst, *Forgiving What You Can't Forget,* 45.

Chapter 7: Who Do You Want to Be?

1. Arden Bevere, *Redefined: Confronting the Labels That Limit Us* (Grand Rapids: Baker, 2021), 9–10.

Chapter 8: The Comparison Killer

1. Steven Furtick, "Stop Comparing Yourself," Official Steven Furtick, September 24, 2019, YouTube video, 12:36, https://www.youtube .com/watch?v=k104U3RQnqo.
2. Jessica Brown, "Is Social Media Bad for You? The Evidence and the Unknowns," BBC, January 4, 2018, https://www.bbc.com/future /article/20180104-is-social-media-bad-for-you-the-evidence-and-the -unknowns.
3. Craig Groeschel, "God Never Said That: Part 1 – 'God Wants You Happy,'" Life.Church, February 9, 2015, YouTube video, 37:21, https://www.youtube.com/watch?v=OmWDuesPTbo.

Chapter 9: Confidence Boost

1. Lisa Bevere, *Girls with Swords: How to Carry Your Cross like a Hero* (Colorado Springs: Waterbrook, 2013), 47.
2. Steven Furtick, "The Source of True Confidence," Official Steven Furtick, July 11, 2017, YouTube video, 4:25, https://www.youtube .com/watch?v=wOoYzgAkaIg.
3. Will Durant, *The Story of Philosophy: The Lives and Opinions of the World's Greatest Philosophers* (1926; repr., New York: Pocket, 2006), 98.
4. "11 Facts about Body Image," DoSomething.org, accessed March 21, 2021, https://www.dosomething.org/us/facts /11-facts-about-body-image#fnref4.
5. "11 Facts about Body Image," DoSomething.org.

Chapter 11: Pressure's On

1. Lisa Bevere, *Girls with Swords: How to Carry Your Cross like a Hero* (Colorado Springs: Waterbrook, 2013), 99.
2. Orrin Woodward in Niall J, "Mind the Gap: 'Pressure Squeezes Effort out of Winners and Excuses out of Losers,' Author Orrin Woodward," Celtic Star, December 20, 2019, https://thecelticstar .com/mind-the-gap-pressure-squeezes-effort-out-of-winners-and -excuses-out-of-losers-author-orrin-woodward/.

Chapter 13: The Fight for Your Moment

1. Sadie Robertson, *Live Original: How the Duck Commander Teen Keeps It Real and Stays True to Her Values* (New York: Howard, 2014), 43.
2. John C. Maxwell (@JohnCMaxwell), "Leadership—When It Matters Most: Focus," April 27, 2020, Facebook video, 44:56, https://www.facebook.com/JohnCMaxwell/videos/leadership-when -it-matters-most-focus/241373660444019/.
3. Craig Groeschel, *Altar Ego: Becoming Who God Says You Are* (Grand Rapids: Zondervan, 2013), 10.